CAUTION

This book contains material that's likely to change your life. Certainly the truths contained within it have changed the lives of many in weekly meetings held by the author. But don't take our word for it. Read what others have said about how God has used the ministry of Victory in Jesus in their lives:

"I was an alcoholic for fifteen years, but Jesus made me a minister of His Gospel. Now I pastor a church in Virginia."
—Wilbert

"When the power of God touched me, I stopped running the biggest crack house in Plainfield, NJ—and started running toward Jesus. Today, I'm a family man."
—Charley

"God showed me cancer and drug addiction are no match for Him. I've been set free from all of them."
—Elaine

"I was on methodone maintenance for 18 years when I found out God wanted me on His maintenance for life. [I was set free from heroin.]"
—Pete

"The smell of crack cocaine ain't nothing compared to the sweet fragrance of Jesus that rescued me from a downward spiral of death—to a seat in heavenly places."
—Larry

For further information on speaking engagements, seminars, and prison ministry, please write:

VICTORY IN JESUS OUTREACH MINISTRIES
P. O. Box 11023
New Brunswick, NJ 08906

VICTORY IN JESUS

Living Answers for a Dying World

Vinny Longo

with Lloyd B. Hildebrand

BRIDGE-LOGOS Publishers
North Brunswick, NJ

All Scripture verses, unless otherwise indicated, are from the King James Version of the Bible.

Victory in Jesus: Living Answers for a Dying World
by Vinny Longo
ISBN: 0-88270-694-2
Library of Congress Catalog Card Number: 96-84794
Copyright © 1996 by **BRIDGE-LOGOS** *Publishers*

Published by:
BRIDGE-LOGOS *Publishers*
North Brunswick Corporate Center
1300 Airport Road, Suite E
North Brunswick, NJ 08902

DEDICATION

We dedicate this book to our children, grandchildren,
and
great-grandchildren—all of whom we love so much.

TABLE OF CONTENTS

Acknowledgments

We acknowledge Pastor David T. DeMola of Faith Fellowship World Outreach Center for the encouragement he has provided over the years. We'll never forget how he taught on Joshua and Asa and inspired us to become courageous warriors for the Lord. Oftentimes unaware of the personal battles we were going through, Pastor DeMola, through the administration of the Holy Spirit, always had a word *in season* for us. He relentlessly urged us to go on no matter what the circumstance appeared to be. Today, we look back on those times, and we thank God for Pastor DeMola. His faith propelled us toward the many victories we've experienced at Victory in Jesus.

We are fruit that remains as a result of his dedication to Christ. The ministry of Victory in Jesus at Faith Fellowship would never have existed without him. We believe our ministry is a success today because we sit under a man of character who overflows with the love of God and the compassion of Jesus for souls. To this day, he encourages everyone to fulfil their calling in God.
Thank you, Pastor DeMola.

Foreword

Like the Apostle Paul, Vinny Longo experienced a radical conversion experience in mid-life. I first met him and his vibrant wife, Nancy, at a diner in South Plainfield, New Jersey. As this extraordinary couple shared their experiences with me, I soon realized that I was sitting with two people whose lives had been totally transformed by God, and whose hearts are now fully focused on serving Him with all their strength.

Strength is the most effective word to use in describing this remarkable pair. As radical followers of Jesus Christ, truly they are "strong in the Lord, and in the power of his might" (Eph. 6:10). The joy of the Lord is their strength. (See Neh. 8:10). Both Vinny and Nancy are valiant warriors in the army of God. They are not ashamed of the Gospel of Jesus Christ, because they know "it is the power of God unto salvation to every one that believeth" (Rom. 1:16).

Their enthusiasm for the things of God, including evangelism and spiritual warfare, is truly contagious. Their knowledge of God's Word and their practical application of the Scriptures are insightful and compelling. Their love for God, each other, and the Body of Christ is vividly genuine.

God has called these special people into a ministry that many would consider to be unglamorous. As Vinny puts it, they minister to "the down-and outers- and the up-and outers." It is their privilege to share the love of God with prostitutes, homosexuals, drug addicts, homeless people, alcoholics, witches, satanists, abuse victims and perpetrators, hopeless individuals, the terminally ill, street kids, AIDS victims, church leaders, business people, clergy, the mentally ill, and countless other victims of the kingdom of darkness. The ministry is known as Victory in Jesus; it is an adjunct to Faith Fellowship, a dynamic church in Edison, New Jersey.

Vinny approaches ministry with a roll-up-your-sleeves and don't-be afraid-to-get-dirty outlook. His energy is boundless. His style is simple and direct. His philosophy is the Bible. He provides answers to the cries of the human heart. The people who come to Victory in Jesus meetings on Friday evenings are filled with hurts, confusion, scars, and questions. Vinny gives them God's answers—the only answers that are able to change the human heart and the effects of sin.

This book is not about Vinny and Nancy, however. Rather, it is about the power of God and His anointing, which breaks every yoke (See Isa. 58:6). It is a book of answers for "down-and-outers" as well as "up-and-outers." The teaching of this book is powerfully prophetic, and it clearly demonstrates what God is doing in our world today. Every pastor, church leader, evangelist, church member, as well as those who need to know the Savior, will find this book to be a clarion call to positive action to stem the tide of iniquity in these last days. This is a battle manual for every spiritual soldier.

The testimonies in this book will inspire you. The anointed teaching will set you free. The call to battle will grip you, and the answers to your questions will keep you focused on all God has in store for you. As you read, be prepared to make immediate changes in your life-style, for you will never be the same after reading this book. Your faith-level in God and in His Word will accelerate beyond all your expectations. Your life in God will become radical.

As a writer and editor, I have worked with many authors and books over several years. Seldom have I felt so strongly impelled to be a part of a writing project as I have felt about *Victory in Jesus*. Its message has the potential to change people, including the Body of Christ, in ways we haven't seen since the publication of *The Cross and the Switchblade* and *Run, Baby, Run*.

Reading this book is a spiritual experience, and its anointing will touch every area of your heart and soul.

Lloyd B. Hildebrand

Introduction

Thanks be to God, which giveth us the
victory through our Lord Jesus Christ.
(1 Cor 15:57)

We Have Good News.

In 1939, Eugene M. Bartlett wrote a hymn that serves to describe the ministry of Victory in Jesus:

I heard an old, old story,
how a Savior came from glory,
How He gave His life on Calvary
to save a wretch like me;
I heard about His groaning of His precious
blood's atoning,
Then I repented of my sins and won the
victory!

This verse is my personal testimony, and it has been the testimony of millions of believers throughout Church history who have found victory in Jesus by trusting Him for salvation. It is Nancy's testimony as well, and as you will see as you read, it has become the anthem of hundreds of men, women, and young people who have attended our services at Victory in Jesus. "And this is the victory that overcometh the world, even our faith" (1 John 5:4).

Without any reservations whatsoever, we believe that God has the power to save to the uttermost all those who come to Him by faith (See Heb 7:25). We preach the Gospel of Jesus Christ to those who attend our meetings, to people in the street, to waitresses, bus drivers, and all we meet. We have learned that Jesus is the only One who can answer the cries of the human heart in permanent and effective ways. We have rejoiced with the angels in heaven time after time as we have led the lost to Christ and reclaimed backsliders. Our ministry is an honor and a joy, even though we have sometimes encountered obstacles along the way.

Since 1960, the national population has increased only forty-one percent, but the number of violent crimes in our nation has increased by more than 500 percent. Truly, lawlessness abounds. The fastest growing segment of the criminal population is our young people, who seem, in many cases, to be adrift on a sea of doubt, confusion, and hopelessness. Poverty is increasing at alarming rates in both urban and rural areas, and millions of children are affected by this increase.

In the 1980s, one out of every ten unwed teen-age girls became pregnant. This alarming trend continues, as does illicit sexual activity among people of all ages. It is predicted that in the very near future (if we are not there already) one million teen-age girls will become pregnant annually, resulting in hundreds of thousands of abortions.

Approximately three million teen-agers contract venereal disease, including AIDS, each year.

At Victory in Jesus, we meet these victims, and it is our privilege to minister the love of God and the power of the Gospel to them. It is such a joy to see them healed, delivered, and completely set free. Evangelism, therefore, is a priority in our calling, because we know that ". . . as many as received him, to them gave he power to become the sons of God, even to them that believe on his name" (John 1:12). This generation needs to hear the Gospel of Jesus Christ, and they need to see its reality unveiled. This is what Victory in Jesus is all about, and this is the central theme of our book as well.

Healing Hands

> *I heard about His healing,*
> *of His cleansing power revealing,*
> *How He made the lame to walk again*
> *and caused the blind to see;*
> *And then I cried, "Dear Jesus,*
> *come and heal my broken spirit,*
> *And somehow Jesus came and brought*
> *me the victory!*

What a privilege it has been for me to watch this verse of Bartlett's song come true before my eyes as I have observed Jesus, the Great Physician, put His power to heal into effect in the lives of AIDS victims, the terminally ill, the addicted, and those who suffer from a broken spirit. I know He is the Healer because He healed me. This is the ministry of the Anointed One, Jesus of Nazareth, and because He lives within each of us who know Him, the power of His anointing is within us. It flows from our innermost being like a river of living water, and it sets captives free. Jesus said, "The Spirit of the Lord is upon me, because he hath anointed me to preach the gospel to the poor; he hath sent me to heal the brokenhearted, to preach deliverance to the captives, and recovering of sight to the blind, to set at liberty them that are bruised" (Luke 4:18).

At Victory in Jesus, we endeavor to follow in the footsteps of our Master by preaching the Gospel of Jesus Christ to those who are poor (both materially and spiritually). God's trophies of grace that have come through our ministry include some from the growing segment of homeless people in our society. Victims of abuse have received the "glorious liberty of the sons of God" through Victory in Jesus. Captives to addictions of all sorts, including drugs, alcohol, sexual problems, and other idolatries, have been set free. The brokenhearted have been healed. "To God be the glory—great things He hath done!"

On the pages of this book you will meet some of these homeless folks, former homosexuals, ex-addicts, recovered (not recovering) alcoholics, as well as people who once felt that they were hopeless because society had branded them as such. You will watch them step out of the kingdom of darkness into the Kingdom of light. You will rejoice with us as you see the power of God unfolding on the pages in front of you.

There is a balm in Gilead that heals the sin-sick soul. Jesus said, ". . . they shall lay hands on the sick, and they shall recover" (Mark 16:18b). We accept this truth as our commission at Victory in Jesus, and we have seen wonderful healings accomplished through the manifest power of God.

Victors, not Victims

I heard about a mansion
He has built for me in glory.
And I heard about the streets of gold
beyond the crystal sea;
About the angels singing
and the old redemption story,
And some sweet day I'll sing up there the
song of victory!

Fortunately, we don't have to wait for heaven before we can sing the song of victory. Those who have been delivered through Victory in Jesus are singing that sweet song every Friday evening at our glorious meetings. The Lord inhabits the praises of His people, and He pours His love upon us. "If the Son therefore shall make you free, ye shall be free indeed" (John 8:36). One of our responsibilities at Victory in Jesus is to help the new convert find this place of spiritual freedom (victory) in Jesus. Through the teaching of the Word of God (our major emphasis) we show each one how to stand fast in that liberty. Our goal is to equip these special people of God for their calling and ministry in the Body of Christ. In the process, we are adding members to the Church of Jesus Christ on a daily basis.

The Apostle wrote, "Stand fast therefore in the liberty wherewith Christ hath made us free, and be not entangled again with the yoke of bondage" (Gal 5:1). Jesus came to break every yoke. His anointing in our lives is the power to deliver those who are oppressed by the enemy. We believe His Word and we stand upon it. We act in accord with His Word. We always endeavor to put His anointed Word into action in the lives we are privileged to serve. Through the power of His anointing and the power of His Word, we have seen hundreds of people learn to stand fast in the liberty God has given to them. In most cases they never return to the yoke of bondage that had kept them in slavery for so long.

As the third verse in Bartlett's hymn "Victory In Jesus" declares, this world is not our home. We are citizens of a different kingdom—the Kingdom of God's love and light. Through the ministry of the Word of God and the power of prayer, we are able to lead many souls out of the kingdom of darkness into His marvelous light (See 1 Peter 2:9).

We reach out to the victims of our society so that they, like us, will be empowered by the Spirit of God to become productive members of the Body of Christ and society-at-large. Many of those we minister to experienced abuse as children, and this has caused their self-image to be shattered. The love of Jesus heals those who suffer from inferiority complexes and shattered self-images.

Dramatic increases in child abuse have been documented for decades in our society. There is a multiple causation behind most of these that has been engineered by the master deceiver—Satan himself. Some of the snares he has used to trip people up include substance abuse, sexual addictions, single parenthood, and other factors—but his goal is always the same: to deceive, accuse, and destroy. Alarming rates of teen-age suicide attest to these realities, and this self-destructive trend has escalated so far as to place suicide as the third leading cause of death among adolescents, after motor vehicle accidents and other accidents. The murder of teen-agers and children is increasing as well, as our young people learn to carry weapons to school.

Less than 60 percent of all children today live with their biological parents. The children of divorce are reeling from all the confusion and adjustments they have to cope with. Through Victory in Jesus, we are able to change the status of these victims as they learn to respond to the love of Jesus and the power of God in their lives. We lay hands on them, and they recover—both from physical and emotional illnesses that have held them back through most of their lives. We reveal to them that such conditions are not God's will for them, and like flowers opening so beautifully in the sunshine of spring, these special people begin to blossom in the sunshine of their Father's love for them.

All we hope to be is the Father's hands extended, reaching out to the oppressed, and like Jesus, our goal is to go about doing good and healing all who are oppressed by the enemy (See Luke 10:19).

Clashing Kingdoms

A warfare rages in our society. The enemy (Satan—the adversary) strives to win the hearts and minds of people everywhere. He has been remarkably successful in doing so. "The thief [Satan] cometh not, but for to steal, and to kill, and to destroy: I am come that they might have life, and that they might have it more abundantly" (John 10:10). This is both bad news and good news. It is bad news to those who reject Jesus, but great joy to those who receive Him. At Victory in Jesus, our ministry involves the spiritual warfare that is necessary to enable an individual to see the truth that will set him or her free. We engage in the battle on their behalf by dethroning the principalities and powers that have controlled them for so many years. We endeavor to expose the works of the prince of darkness and his emissaries (See Rom. 13:12).

We teach our people to put on the whole armor of God (See Eph. 6). We show them how to wage warfare as good soldiers of Jesus Christ who walk in the light and love of God and His Word. We help them to see that their minds need to be renewed by the washing in the water of God's Word (See Eph. 4:23).

We have included some of this teaching in the pages of our book so that you can better understand the approach we take. It is our hope that by doing so you will be renewed in the spirit of your mind as well and that you will be better equipped to wage spiritual warfare in your particular sphere. In doing so, we must always keep in mind that, ". . . we wrestle not against flesh and blood, but against principalities, against powers, against the rulers of the darkness of this world, against spiritual wickedness in high places" (Eph. 6:12). Satan can only be in one place at a time, but his agents are everywhere, doing their fiendish works. Through the ministry of Victory in Jesus, we ascertain who that true enemy is, and we go after him with a vengeance on behalf of the ones he has victimized. God is always with us in the battle, and He will be with you as well.

Much of this teaching is included in our book, and it is our prayer that as you read, you will see the truths of God's Word in an entirely new light—a light so radiant and powerful that it will lead you to change the way you look at everything in your life, including God, yourself, other people, and the circumstances that surround you. We ask you to pray for us as well, and for each of those people who find victory in Jesus at our meetings.

> *O victory in Jesus, my Savior, forever!*
> *He sought me and bought me with His*
> *redeeming blood;*
> *He loved me ere I knew Him, and all my love*
> *is due Him—*
> *He plunged me to victory beneath the*
> *cleansing flood.*

God loves you, and He wants you to find that victory in Jesus that is your rightful inheritance as a child of God. My only regret is that it took me so long to discover it for myself, but once I found it (as you will see in chapter one), I was never the same again. Open yourself to all God has for you as you read these pages, and I can assure you that you will never be the same again!

Vinny Longo
Edison, New Jersey
September, 1995

1

The Night Watch

Twas grace that taught my heart to fear,
And grace my fears relieved;
How precious did that grace appear
The hour I first believed!
(John Newton)

The Dark Night of the Soul

He looked like a prisoner at Dachau because he was so emaciated, blotched, lined, old-looking, but he was only twenty-five. John had attended our Victory in Jesus meetings several times. He had given his life to Jesus who had freed him from his heroin enslavement. I remember how John had once said, " I used to be in the dregs of drug abuse, but Jesus has set me free!" How we had all rejoiced with him—but that was three years earlier.

John had failed to stand fast in the liberty wherewith Christ had set him free, and he chose rather to become entangled once more with "that yoke of bondage" (See Gal. 5:1).

This precious young man, once so on fire for God, had fallen prey to the enemy of his soul. He had surrendered to the familiar powers of darkness that were clearly out to destroy him. The spirit of drug abuse had made certain to work overtime on John, trying to convince him that he was enslaved forever. But God who can sustain and maintain anything that's His, had another plan for John. "No one shall snatch them away from me for my Father has given them to me and He is more powerful than anyone else. No one can kidnap them from me" (See John 10: 28-29, paraphrased).

As Nancy and I approached our friend in the hospital room, I felt a sense of indescribable sorrow and sadness. We hadn't seen him for a couple of years. The more I thought about it, I realized that righteous anger was the emotion behind my grieving. Nancy and I clutched each other's hand very tightly as we turned the dark corridor of the depressing hospital ward. The familiar antiseptic smell of hospitals filled our nostrils as we glanced up together and had our first shocking look at John. He was a skeleton covered with a thin layer of paper-like skin. Purple lesions from Karposi's sarcoma dotted his arms, legs, and face. We stopped and took a deep breath.

Regaining our composure, Nancy said, " John, it's Vinny and Nancy from Victory in Jesus. Do you remember us?"

The barely breathing corpse in front of us nodded his recognition of our names. His young eyes were more like the dim eyes of an elderly person with cataracts than the vibrant eyes of the John we once knew. "Jesus loves you, John," I reminded him.

He nodded once more.

"Let us pray for you, brother," I offered. "Lord God, we know you love John, and we know you want him to be with you forever in heaven. Eventhough he turned his back on you, we know that your mercy and loving kindness is endless and that you're quick to forgive. So we ask for this mercy for John, so that he will know that he has eternal life with you in heaven."

Then Nancy asked, "John, will you repeat these words after us?"

His dry voice responded with a weak yes, and we led him in a prayer of rededication. We knew John had not continued to walk in the free gift of healing that God had provided for him. We had heard from his friends that he had willingly turned back to an active life of drug abuse even though he had tasted the grace of God. Though Nancy and I could not truly understand then why he had chosen such a path, we knew that God still loved John—and so did we.

While my wife led him in a prayer of rededication, John responded with weak whispers and nods. We knew that God had heard his prayer. As the Apostle John wrote, "Now this is the confidence that we have in Him, that if we ask anything according to His will, He hears us. And if we know He hears us, whatever we ask, we know that we have the petitions that we have asked of Him" (1 John 5:14-15, NKJV).

Standing on either side of John's hospital bed, Nancy and I held his cold, lifeless hands as we prayed. After saying amen, we looked into his eyes. They sparkled with new life, and a faint smile could be detected on his parched and cracked lips. It seemed as if his face was proclaiming hope and faith, which enabled him to transcend the pain and nausea if only for a moment. We knew that John would soon go to heaven to be with Jesus. We leaned over and kissed his cheeks. A tiny tear emerged from the corner of his eye and coursed down his gray and purple face. John had been reclaimed!

On our way home, Nancy and I talked about our friend. We felt we had won a battle, but had lost the war. It was so discouraging to realize that the enemy had snatched another life out of our hands!

For almost five years we had ministered to the lost. We had seen many miracles in response to our proclamation of the Gospel and our teaching of God's Word, but in spite of these realities, Nancy and I were engaged in the most tumultuous spiritual battle we had ever faced. The year was 1989, and I felt as if I were on the verge of "throwing in the towel."

"What's the use, Honey? We work so hard, but it seems as if everything we work for goes right down the drain. John is going to die soon, and Joann just died of cancer. Why is this happening? What are we doing wrong?"

Nancy was quiet for a long time as we continued our drive along U.S. Route 22, past all the mattress and dinette shops, the diners, the shopping centers, department stores, and fast-food places. She reached over and took my hand, and without saying anything, she began to weep. "Let's pull over and pray," she suggested.

Good advice, I thought. "God, I thank you for giving me such a sweet and sensitive helpmate," I prayed silently. The parking lot of a K-mart served our purpose nicely. I parked the car under a tall light and began to pray, "Heavenly Father, what is this all about? Why are we losing so many of the people we've taught and loved through the years? Help us to see what we need to change." I began to weep, and Nancy's tears mingled with mine. It was difficult to lose so many battles to the enemy of our souls, but in our heart of hearts, we knew this was not God's will for us—or for those we loved and served.

In the space of only one year, we had lost three people to AIDS, one to cancer, one to suicide, and several to drugs. It seemed almost too much to bear. Where had we gone wrong? Those whom Jesus had set free had willingly returned to bondage. Why?

"Nancy, I must not be in the right place. I must be trying to do something I'm not called to do. I feel like getting out of this nightmare!"

"No, Vinny, God is going to see us through. Things are going to get better. You wait and see."

The counsel of my beautiful wife was not enough for me that night. Prayer was not enough. The former victories were not enough. I was so discouraged I was ready to quit. I knew that something was missing, something that only God knew and only God could give to me. I knew I had to have a fresh anointing, a new direction from God to enable me to carry on and go forward in His work. I admitted to myself that what I was doing wasn't working the way God wanted it to work, and I knew the instructions for change had come from Him alone.

As soon as we got home the phone rang. It was John's sister. "John died at 9:00 this evening. I thought you would want to know." Just two hours after we had prayed for him! "It's too much, Lord! I can't take it." Bitter tears found their course down my cheeks. "Is this what you want me to do?"

Even though I didn't feel like it, I went before the Lord to seek Him. I determined in my heart that I would spend time with Him for the answers I knew only He could give me. I would wait on Him for His wisdom. I was so tired of all the failures and of seeing all the defeat, and I knew that without His intervention, my only option would be to get in touch with some of my friends in the business world and see if they could get me a secular job. It was a crucial moment at a crossroads between continued commitment and comfort. I needed for God to show me what to do.

Born Dead

My parents, like so many of the families in Newark, New Jersey, in the twenties, were Italian immigrants. They were devout Roman Catholics who went to confession and attended Mass as often as they could. My mother, Donatina LaStella, was from Avalino, Italy, and my father, Philip Longo, came from Sicily. They emigrated to America hoping for a new life that would be filled with glorious opportunities.

It must have been very exciting for them to anticipate the birth of their first child—me! If the baby was a boy, they determined, he would be named Vincent, after the French saint who taught his followers to unite themselves to Jesus by clinging to Him. Vincent de Paul was a deeply spiritual priest whose mystical life of prayer led many into the Kingdom of God.

As the time for my delivery drew near, excitement mounted in the hearts of the young Italian couple who were to become my parents. The contractions told them it was time to go to the hospital, and soon I would make my first appearance into the world—dead.

The nurse left the delivery room and went to my father who was waiting nervously for news concerning his young bride and his first-born child. She sat down next to him in the waiting room and said, "Mr. Longo, your wife had a little boy, but he died. I'm so sorry to have to tell you this."

Something happened to my twenty-two-year-old father when he heard that. He didn't believe it. Something welled up inside of him that made him refuse to accept her word.

"I want to see the baby," he demanded.

Hesitantly, the nurse escorted him into the delivery room. "Let me see the baby," he told the doctor.

The obstetrician commanded the nurse to take me from the little black basket and to put me on the table. He was going to show my father that I was truly lifeless.

As the nurse lifted me by my feet, however, I began to bellow and scream like a newborn piglet. Immediately, they put an oxygen mask over my red face and the stunned doctor and nurse gave me their undivided attention. My father was immensely joyous and proud to discover that his first-born child was not dead after all. It was my dad's first act as my advocate, and if he had not intervened immediately, I would not be here today. His persistent faith paid off, for I was very much alive in spite of the doctor's pronouncement to the contrary.

God had a plan for my life. My godly grandmother had prophesied over my mother when she was carrying me, "This baby will be a boy. He will become a priest."

"I Should Have Left You in the Basket!"

I was the first of four sons. Though our church taught that original sin had been wiped away at our baptisms, we often found ourselves in the midst of mayhem and mischief. I loved to tease my brothers and my mother. There were many times when she would playfully respond to my teasing by saying, " I should have left you in the basket!"

Times were difficult for the Longos during the Great Depression. My parents worked hard to provide for us, but it seemed we could never get ahead. Their lives were filled with tension as they endeavored "to keep the wolf away from the door." At the end of the Depression, my father went back into the construction trade. He was an honest, hard-working man.

7

My mother was a wonderful cook. She loved her family and always tried to make life sweet and pleasant for us. Her sweet tomato sauce made us wrinkle our toes. It possessed an aroma and flavor that I can still smell and taste. Pasta seemed to be a part of every meal, and her home-baked breads and pastries helped to fill the hungry void in the stomachs of her boys. Mama loved to cook, and no meal in the world could match her spaghetti with meatballs accompanied with garlic bread. Her Italian cookies were the sweetest delicacies in the whole world. Getting her husband and four growing sons to eat her home-cooking was never a problem.

As the years passed, dad prospered in the construction and transportation fields, and we boys worked with him after school and on weekends. Later, each one of us began driving trucks for him. Eventually, three corporations grew out of the Longo Trucking Firm, which flourished beyond our expectations. We transported chemicals needed by the petroleum industry upon which America's lifeline of production and transportation flowed.

We learned so much from our hard-working parents. They maintained their Catholic faith through difficult circumstances. My brothers and I, however, began to drift away from the church. Our growing prosperity as a family enabled us to enjoy some of the things this world has to offer, and we became content with worldy pursuits, totally neglecting the spiritual part of our lives.

I loved cars, girls, dancing, and drinking—perhaps in that order - and I was an athlete. I played football and boxed. In my late teens, I stopped going to church altogether, much to my mother's chagrin. To me, church and faith and Jesus were for old ladies and sissies. This error in my thinking continued until I was middle-aged.

"I Don't Want to Die!"

God broke through the haze of my selfishness and worldliness as I was driving with Rocco Molinaro, my life-long buddy from school. We were transporting chemicals from the Dow Corporation in our eighteen-wheel tanker from Midland, Michigan, to Hoboken, New Jersey, when the totally unexpected happened.

I had taught Rocco how to drive, and he always seemed to be extremely cautious and attentive. He had a wife and eight children to provide for, so he always worked hard and conscientiously. But on this morning he seemed unusually tired and irritable.

Rocco was a huge man who weighed nearly 250 pounds. We shared many memories of our "coming of age" in school. Rocco had always been my buddy—we played football together, fought together, drank together, and partied together. In many ways, we were inseparable. And now we were working together.

As we were traveling on Route 10 out of Midland, we saw the signs for I-75 at Bay City, Michigan. Uncharacteristically, Rocco went into the entrance at a high rate of speed. I don't know whether the entrance came upon him more suddenly than he realized, or if he was too tired to react promptly, but for whatever reason, we hurtled into the sharp curve that led to the interstate at a speed that must have exceeded fifty miles per hour. I tensed up immediately, because I knew that there was no way that Rocco could maneuver his 80,000-pound rig at such a speed through such a sharp turn. I yelled, "We're going over!"

Rocco gripped the steering wheel as if to brace himself against the inevitable. I fell over toward him as the tanker flipped over like a huge aircraft falling from the sky. The tanker flipped onto its side, skidding and violently plowing into the shoulder dirt for more than 300 feet. It was a time of total helplessness.

I sensed a thick, impenetrable darkness coming over our cab like a shroud thrown over us by some unknown power in the air. I tried to push the dense darkness away. I felt as if I was falling into it—there was no time to think, to pray, to talk, to plan, to move. We were in the hands of a force that was beyond our control.

I started to fall into the darkness, and these were my only words: "I don't want to die, God! I don't want to die!" It all seemed so empty, however, as if the words were only echoes of some forgotten prayer. The silence was broken only by the fear that gripped our hearts. It would soon be over.

A few moments later, I came to my senses, but somehow I found myself outside of the vehicle lying on my stomach next to the twisted truck. It was mangled as if a giant's hands had crushed it in the same way a human might destroy a beverage can. As my vision cleared, I saw Rocco's arm sticking out of the tangled heap of metal. The silence was deafening, and I wished his arm would move or that he would call out for help, but there was no sound.

Had the truck not spaded the earth like a bulldozer, creating a mound of dirt preventing us from sliding further, we would have been hurtled down a steep embankment into a water resevoir. I wondered if Rocco could possibly be alive, but as I tried to get up, excruciating pain gripped my back like the clenching jaws of a vise. I could not move and nearly fainted. I put my head back on the ground and tried to breathe deeply in an effort to stave off the pain and the threatening loss of consciousness.

As I lay there, I almost passed out from the fumes of the diesel fuel that was forming a puddle in the very spot where my face was lying. It scared me, because I thought it might catch fire and explode the truck, Rocco, and me.

A passerby must have reported the accident to the authorities, because an ambulance soon arrived. I was carefully placed on a stretcher and rushed to the hospital. The orthopedic surgeon who examined me was very straightforward as he said, "You have completely fractured your L-2 vertebrae. Though you are very close to needing an operation, I am choosing not to operate for now. We'll have to wait and see how it does. You will need a metal cast, however."

"Well, doc," I said weakly. "How's my friend?"

"I haven't heard . . ."

Another man walked through the door. The nurse introduced him as the coroner. He came over to my bed and said, "I'm sorry to have to tell you your friend didn't make it. He was killed instantly. His body was mangled beyond recognition."

Guilt and remorse far more painful than my physical condition filled my heart and soul. "I made it, but Rocco didn't," I thought. Why? The shock turned to anger. "Why, God? Why did Rocco have to die?"

That night in the hospital something very strange occurred. It was about 1:30 in the morning. A woman, a young man, and a child entered my room. They were smiling. "We know you feel badly about losing your friend. We want you to know that everything will be all right."

Indescribable peace and comfort filled my breast. How did they know I was worried about him and his family? Who were they?

The next morning I asked my nurse, "Who were the people that visited me last night?"

She laughed as she answered, "What people? You couldn't have had any visitors. The hospital is locked as tight as a drum after midnight."

The Night Grows Darker

As the years passed, the pain, hurt, and turmoil continued to grow. In many ways I was bitter toward God for all that had happened—the accident, the loss of my best friend, my pain and injury. My health was declining, and so was our business. Longo Trucking, once a very prosperous company, began to decline, as did the petroleum industry itself. These declines were taking place at a steady rate during the seventies.

Simultaneously, my marriage was showing signs of fatigue. My wife and I had five beautiful children. My bitterness and resentment, however, had worked against my having a good relationship with anyone. My first marriage eventually ended in a bitter divorce. Soon thereafter, I married another woman and we had a new baby.

By 1978, our company was forced to go out of business. The collapse destroyed four families—my parents, my own family, and the families of two of my brothers. We were down and out in a way that we had not known since the Great Depression.

During the fifties and sixties, we had been able to enjoy many luxuries: Nice cars, beautiful homes, summer vacations at the Jersey Shore, trips throughout the U.S., splendid clothing, and many other of life's "finer things." My focus was on money, and I was selfishly involved in the pursuit of riches and materialism. I was so selfish, in fact, that I was not able to truly love other people—and certainly not God. The only time I went to church was for weddings and funerals, and I tried to avoid those as often as I possibly could!

Once a prosperous businessman who had sat on the boards of three corporations, I was now reduced to the status of a divorced, middle-aged man who was looking for a job. My leg was really bothering me as a result of my back injury. The doctors in New Jersey had agreed with the Michigan surgeon by saying that surgery was not indicated in my case, because an operation might make matters worse. It was their belief that the L-2 fracture of my spine would build a protective callus around itself, but I would lose about one-third of my ability to bend. Surgery would provide a 50-50 chance of recovery, but it could also cause further damage. They predicted that the spinal injury would result in the loss of reflexes in my legs. They were certainly right about this, because by 1980 all the reflexes in my left leg were gone. The doctor would strike the spot below my left knee with his rubber-tipped hammer and nothing would happen. The sciatic-lumbar region was deteriorating.

It made me angry that I had to face such limitations in my own life. Always before I had been as strong as an ox, now I would sometimes stumble as I walked. My financial success had seemed so certain, but now the bottom had dropped out of my life. The important areas of faith and family had taken a back seat in my life, and I regrettably realized that I had failed in these areas as well. It was a dark time indeed.

"What's going to happen next?" I would often wonder. I've lost my wife, my money, my job, and my hope. It can't get any worse." But I was wrong. It seemed as if calamity had found a home in my life and family.

"The Lord Has Healed You!"

In my desperate search for security (in all the wrong places), I failed to spend any quality time with my new wife

and children. There seemed to be only one place to turn—
my brother Joe in Phoenix, Arizona. The Sun Belt sounded
like a nice place to live. I knew the area was growing, and I
felt certain that Joe might be able to help me find a job there.
Was a sunny new beginning just around the corner?

Late in 1979, I called Joe. "How're you doing?" I
inquired to my younger brother.

"Just fine, Vinny. How are you?"

I had too much pride to tell Joe everything, but I did
manage to ask if I could come for a visit in the hopes of
securing a job.

"Certainly, brother. I've been expecting you."

It hit me with the force of a lightning bolt. What did he
mean by "I've been expecting you?" The words echoed in
my mind throughout the weeks preceding my visit to Arizona.

I arrived in the beautiful Southwest early in January, 1980.
The first question I asked Joe was, "What did you mean when
you said, 'I've been expecting you.'?"

With a sparkle in his eye and a faint smile on his lips, he
responded, "I've been praying for you, Vinny."

We all knew that Joe had become a "born-again
Christian," a phrase that we had heard in connection with the
Jimmy Carter campaign, but we had no idea what it meant.
We had all assumed that Joe had become a religious fanatic
of some sort, and now I was convinced of it!

"God has answered my prayer, Vinny. I've been praying
for you, mama, dad, and our brothers. I'm interceding for
you with prayer and fasting. God told me to start with my
oldest brother first, so I've been focusing my prayers on you."

"Well, okay," I weakly acknowledged. I knew absolutely
nothing about the power of prayer. All I knew was that Joe
called himself a Christian and that he attended a large church
called something like Gospel Echoes in Phoenix. That was

all fine, I reasoned, for him, but I felt that such a life was not for me. What interested me about Joe was the fact that he was involved in the construction business, was well-connected, and I felt certain that he could find a job for me.

That weekend Joe invited me to attend church with him. He mentioned that someone who had once been involved in secular music, a songwriter who had written for stars like Elton John, would be performing in the church. This sounded moderately interesting to me, so I agreed to attend church with my younger brother.

Before announcing the songwriter, the minister (Pastor McHatten) preached. I was not prepared for this, because I had been deliberately trying to avoid any encounter with God for many years. I felt I could handle the music, maybe even a testimony, but the thought of enduring a sermon seemed truly overwhelming to me. Nonetheless, I sat there and listened. It was all so new to me. There was no ritual, no statues, no incense, no candles. The minister spoke with great conviction, and he approached his congregation in a very informal manner. He seemed to glow with love and compassion, and I found myself being attracted to his peaceful, comfortable style.

In the middle of his sermon, Pastor McHatten began to move among the congregation. He walked up and down the center aisle, sometimes moving into certain pews and touching people as he prayed for them. He seemed to know what every member of his congregation suffered from and knew what to pray for them without asking them.

"I hope he doesn't come to me," I thought, as nervous beads of perspiration emerged on my brow. If my statement was a prayer, God did not choose to answer it in the way I wanted Him to, because right then the pastor walked directly toward me, raised his index finger and pointed it straight at me. If he had pointed a gun between my eyes I would not have been more intimidated than I was at that moment. He looked right into my eyes and stated, "You have been in a bad accident. You injured your lower back. God is healing you right now. Stand up and receive your healing!"

I just wasn't used to being singled out in church, and I was embarrassed by this public display. Paranoia began to get the best of me and I thought, "Joe must have told him about my accident." I turned to my sister-in-law who was sitting between me and Joe, "What did Joe do? Tell him about my accident?"

"No, Vinny," she calmly answered. "The Lord has healed you!"

A Little Light Emerges

The next day was my first day on a job Joe had managed to arrange for me. I was hired as a construction worker in the firm of my brother's friend. I was building concrete floors. For the first time in years I felt exhilarated. I felt like tons had been lifted from my shoulders. "Must be the beautiful, sunny Arizona weather," I surmised.

Then I noticed something that had been too wonderful to imagine during all those years since the accident. I could bend over without any pain at all. I felt strong. The pain in my legs was gone. My body felt young and flexible.

"This climate is the best thing in the world for me," I told myself. "This is where I will stay."

Back at the house that evening, I went into the bathroom to take my shower. I decided I would experiment with my physical capabilities by bending over to touch my toes. I did so, and there was no pain! Then it hit me. The meeting! Could it be that God had reached down and touched my body? Was it really possible? Did God tell the pastor to single me out and pray for me?

Fear struck at the core of my being. Such a preposterous idea went against all the self-sufficiency and pride that had served as my foundation for so many years. What's happening to me? Am I going crazy?

I knew the ultimate test of my healing would be found in sitting down and crossing my left leg over my right leg in order to test my reflexes which had been non-existent for many years. Cautiously, I did exactly that. With a hammer chop I brought the edge of my right hand down on the spot just beneath my left knee. My leg jumped! I could feel the nerve as it was struck by my hand. It was unbelievable! I was healed.

Memories of the church service flooded my mind. Bits and pieces of the pastor's sermon came back to me. Throughout that night, the next day, and the next evening, I was literally bombarded by thoughts about the supernatural. The more I thought, the more excited I became—so excited, in fact, that I couldn't breathe, and I even wondered if I was experiencing a heart attack! There was a sensation of pressure within my chest.

All I could think was either I am going crazy or I am dying.

An Unforgettable Presence

In the middle of that Tuesday night, I saw an eerie glow emerge from a corner of the bedroom. It expanded ever so slowly until the entire room was flooded with light. It was not a blinding radiance, but more like a soft glow. It was beautiful. It was peaceful. It was calm.

No sooner did the room fill with light than a replay of my life began to fill my mind and touch my heart. Things that had long been buried resurfaced within me. I began to cry uncontrollably. As the bad memories of sins I had committed appeared before the eyes of my spirit, I confessed them to

God. I told Him that I now realized that my life-style for so many years had been wrong. I had hurt so many people, including my wives and children. I had always wanted to party. I had committed fornication and adultery. I had drank heavily. I had gambled. When I was a truck driver, I had even used drugs in order to stay alert and awake on cross-country drives along monotonous interstates. Like many of my fellow-drivers, I used amphetamines to keep me up, alcohol to bring me down, and women to keep me excited. I was a user of people. I abused others. Everything in my world had been for me alone.

For the first time in my life, I realized that I was the problem in both of my marriages. I asked God to forgive me for the way I treated my first wife, Viola. She was a good woman; I was the problem. Now I found myself grieving over the way our divorce had affected my oldest son, Philip, who was now eighteen. I felt remorse for being a poor father. I had never been there for my kids. My daughters were so beautiful, and now I realized that I had missed their growing up. My oldest daughter, Donna, was now sixteen; I knew she had always wanted to be a doctor, and I wondered if I had discouraged her in this dream. Her sister Debbie was twelve, and I knew she was having a hard time over the break-up of my marriage to Viola. Then there was little three-year-old Gail who no longer had a father!

"God, please forgive me for my hardness of heart," I wept. "I've been a terrible husband and father. I've broken the hearts of my wives and children, and I know I've greatly disappointed my own parents." It was the first time I remember having wept in my entire adulthood, and the tears seemed so helpful. It was as if I was being cleansed from the inside out—and it was wonderful. I felt lighter and happier than I had ever felt. As I brought each sin into the light, honestly confessing it to God and myself, it seemed to lift from my heart and to be replaced by a love I had never experienced.

This macho man who felt he needed no one but himself was beginning to break in response to the grace of God. My lack of compassion was being replaced by the love of God. Formerly people had not meant much to me. I had used them for what I wanted. Now, instead of seeing them as objects for me to use, I saw them as beautiful creations of God. The transition was powerful. I knew it was deep, and I sensed that it was permanent.

After this spiritual catharsis was over, I fell asleep. It was the soundest, most peaceful sleep I had ever experienced. When I awoke the next morning, everything was aglow. I saw everything and everyone from a new point of view. Even when I went to the bathroom mirror and glanced at my face, the radiance of my countenance was so bright that it literally threw me against the wall! It was as if I had been transfigured, and I stood there stunned, staring at the unrecognizable face in the mirror. Who was this man in the mirror? It was a Vinny I had never known before.

All of life was aglow.

Radical for Jesus

I knew I had been with Jesus. I knew that the Great Physician had healed my soul and body. I knew there was a purpose for my life. Immediately, I immersed myself in the Scriptures. I began by reading the Old Testament and the New Testament simultaneously. I was conscious that God was constantly drawing me closer to himself.

It had taken me fifty years, but I knew I had finally discovered the truth. I knew that Jesus Christ was the way, the truth and the life, and I realized that no one could come unto the Father except through Him (See John 14:6). I had lost my home, my business, and several other properties, but I had found my Lord and Savior, Jesus Christ.

The next weekend I flew back to New Jersey in order to gather up our remaining belongings and to move the family to Arizona. My two stepdaughters, Renee and Kim, and my daughter Bridget would be moving with me and my wife to Phoenix, where I now had a good job working in the construction of the Palo Verde Nuclear Plant. At that time, this project was considered to be the biggest construction job in the world.

Upon arriving home, I sat down with my wife, Nina, and shared my testimony with her. She listened attentively but did not ask any questions. In fact, she showed no visible reaction to my witness whatsoever.

Not too many weeks later, my wife, Renee, Kim, and Bridget were all saved and we were baptized in water. At the time of her baptism a man looked at Bridget and prophesied, "The Lord is speaking to you. Because of your beauty, you will walk away from Me. But I will interrupt all your pleasures until you come back to Me."

It turned out to be a true word from the Lord. Months later, after Bridget had wandered away from Jesus, a chiropractor in Ohio who was treating her for a back condition prayed, "In the name of Jesus Christ of Nazareth, guide my hands as I work on Bridget's back."

Startled, my daughter asked, "Do you know my father?"

A decade or so later, Bridget and her entire family came back to Jesus. God's miraculous hand was paving the way for her.

I soon became foreman on the construction job, and I was earning good money. Men from a variety of backgrounds were working under me. Charlie, a Frenchman, responded to my outspoken witness by telling me that he would play devil's advocate for me. I wore "Jesus is Lord" on my hard hat. I was not ashamed of the Gospel of Jesus Christ, because I knew what He had done for me could be the answer for everyone I came in contact with. I became a radical Christian, a follower of Christ who witnessed about Him constantly. I guess people thought I was a fanatic, but I did not care.

As I witnessed to others, Charlie would often mock me in the background. Though I did not like his behavior, I knew I needed to be patient with him, because I felt that God was already at work in his life.

Before Christmas that year, the superintendent announced that we would draw names from a hat the week before Christmas so that we could get presents for each other. We were working in tunnels some thirty feet under the ground at the time. As we emerged from the tunnels each day for lunch on the surface, I would often spend the time by preaching the Gospel to the seven-to-ten men who worked with me.

On one of these lunch breaks, I looked at Charlie and said, 'If I draw your name . . ."

"Stop right there," he interrupted. "If you buy me a Bible, I won't accept it!"

As I drove home that evening I prayed, "Father, I'd like to pick Charlie's name for the Christmas drawing so I can buy him a Bible."

When the time for the drawing arrived, we all went up to the Quonset hut where the superintendent had his office. I sat down next to the shop steward in order to witness to him as the superintendent passed the hat for the drawing of names. When our boss got in front of the shop steward, I glanced over at Charlie who was sitting across the room from me. Our eyes connected. It seemed as if he was glaring at me as I reached into the hat.

I took the paper from the hat without looking at it and walked over to Charlie. I showed him the name on the paper. The hard look on his face changed into a peaceful expression, and then Charlie looked at me and said, "I'll accept it and read it and cherish it for the rest of my life."

Soon after Christmas Charlie became a Christian who was truly able to keep Christmas in his heart each day of the year.

It was one of many times when I witnessed the hand of God moving right in front of me, pouring out His love on people. What an adventure it is to be led by the Spirit of God! That evening God spoke to me on the way home, *"I am the Lord your God and I never change."*

God continues to speak to me in this personal way. His voice is a gentle, peaceful voice that I hear in my spirit. My heavenly Father turned my darkness into dawn, and now He was changing the dawn to noontime. How great it was to walk in the sunshine of God's love.

2

Walking in the Light

Twas grace that taught my heart to fear,
And grace my fears relieved.
How precious did that grace appear,
The hour I first believed.

(John Newton)

A New Beginning

I met Jesus when I was fifty years old. It had taken me a half-century—five decades—to discover that He is the Lord and Savior of my life.

The somber, somewhat frightening figure I had encountered on the crucifixes on the walls at church and in my parents' home had been so distant, so unapproachable. He was dead. How could I ever relate to Him?

I knew His name was Jesus and I knew He had died on a cross, but until I was fifty years old I never knew that He was my risen Savior—the only man who had ever broken the bonds of death. Likewise, I had never known He had died for me!

It was warm and sunny in Arizona—in more ways than one. At my brother's church, Jesus had reached down and touched my life. He healed the problems in my back and leg, but more importantly, Jesus healed my dying spirit.

He replaced my self-righteous pride with the realization that I need Him continually. He replaced my sinfulness with a fervent desire to please Him. He replaced my bondage to Mammon with an earnest devotion to His will.

Jesus' words became the theme of my life: "But seek ye first the Kingdom of God, and His righteousness, and all these things shall be added unto you" (Matt. 6:33).

Jesus had become all in all to me. He had revealed himself as the answer to my every problem. This wonderful knowledge filled me with a joy that was unspeakable, yet I felt a deep need to try and share Him with every person I met. I endeavored to put my experience into words so that others would be able to find their needs met in Jesus as I had done.

Now I knew what Joe had meant when he said he had been born again. There is no better metaphor to use in describing the metamorphosis that takes place when a person receives Jesus Christ as his or her Savior and Lord. It truly is a new birth.

I was a new creation in Christ Jesus. So new, in fact, that I felt that I could hardly recognize myself. I looked differently, talked differently, walked differently, lived differently, wanted different things, had new interests, and felt fully alive for the first time since I was a child. The old Vinny had passed away—died, kicked the bucket, checked out—and the new Vinny was born!

"Therefore if any man be in Christ, he is a new creature: old things are passed away; behold, all things are become new" (2 Cor. 5:17). Life was new for me—everything was different. It was incredibly wonderful.

I had been washed clean. I felt clean. My heart was light. My joy was overflowing. I lived in an atmosphere of love, expectancy, and faith. I could not wait to see what God was going to do next. I was a liberated man. Nothing could hold me back. I felt I was making true progress for the first time in my life. I was renewed, transformed, and recreated. I felt like a little baby nestled in the arms of Jesus. For the first time in my life I felt safe. The worries and fears, and the bad conscience, were gone.

"There is no fear in love; but perfect love casteth out fear: because fear hath torment. He that feareth is not made perfect in love" (1 John 4:18).

Arizona—the name literally means "arid zone." Though it seldom rains there and much of the state is like a desert, I discovered flowing streams of life there. Springs in the desert had washed me clean. Rivers of living water flowed in Arizona, and I was happy to plunge into them with all my might. The water of life had slaked the thirst of my parched soul.

The light that had filled my room there in Joe's house was now filling my soul, and I was learning, step-by-step, how to walk in the light of God's love and truth. I literally devoured the Word of God, and I went to church every time the doors were open.

God Has a Plan for My Life

It thrilled me to see several members of my family come to a saving knowledge of Jesus Christ after I gave my heart to Him. My parents, my wife, my brothers, and some of my children accepted Him.

I told everyone about this One who had given me a new purpose for living. I was a healed and forgiven man, and I was determined to let the whole world know what had happened to me!

For two years I worked at the Palo Verde Nuclear Plant. I enjoyed my work there, earned an excellent salary, but deep within I knew there had to be something more for me.

Nina, my second wife, had left me, and though our broken marriage was very painful for me, I chose to claim God's promise. Instead of trying to figure things out, I stood on His word: "For I know the plans I have for you, 'declares the Lord,' plans to prosper you and not to harm you, plans to give you hope and a future" (Jer. 29:11, NIV).

After I became a Christian, my mother reminded me of grandmother's prophecy that she gave before I was born: "This child will be a boy, and he will be a priest." For the first time in my life, this familiar prophecy had become good news to me! As a young boy and a teen-ager, becoming a priest had seemed to be the worst of all possibilities to me. Now the idea of being a minister of the Gospel of Jesus Christ—a priest of God's Word—sounded wonderful.

In the final analysis, a priest is one who teaches God's Word to the people as he stands positioned between God and man. In some ways, I was already functioning in this role because I would tell almost everyone—including strangers—about Jesus Christ.

Though I tried to deny it by avoiding the thought, I felt an inkling that God might want me to return to my native New Jersey. It was my original home, but the sprawling megalopolis between New York City and the Delaware River did not hold the appeal for me that it once held.

Nonetheless, memory pictures of the "Garden State" (New Jersey) kept flashing in my mind. It took awhile to see these pictures clearly, because so many bad memories of wrongdoing from my past were associated with New Jersey. I remembered the hustle and bustle of life there—and the spiritual darkness that seemed to pervade the chemically polluted atmosphere.

Had it been left to me to decide, I would never have left the warm, sunny environment of Arizona that had become my home in more ways than one. All my Christian friends lived there. Arizona was where I met my Savior, and it was where I learned to worship God with all my heart.

New Jersey, on the other hand, was where I had learned to lie, to cheat, to gamble, to drink, and to use others. Arizona was where I had given all that up in order to love and serve Jesus and His people.

New Jersey was where I had failed in so many areas— as a businessman, a husband, and a father. Arizona was where I had discovered the true meaning of success.

Once I had talked to a Christian brother in Arizona about my desire to be successful, and he had admonished me, "What is this talk about success? You are a failure to begin with. Always remember, without Jesus you cannot do anything but fail."

His words spoke volumes to my heart.

The general impression I had received was that I was definitely to return back East. At first, I hoped this meant North Carolina where my first wife, five children, and ten grandchildren lived. Surely, I reasoned, that is where God wants me to be.

Exactly two years from my first day of work at the Palo Verde plant, on April 5, 1982, I pulled up stakes from the soil of Arizona in response to God's leading. I felt somewhat like Abraham whom God had directed, "Get thee out of thy country . . . unto a land that I will shew thee" (Gen 12:1).

It was like a spiritual adventure to me. God was telling me to go back East, and I was happy to do so. My commitment was to go wherever He would lead me. I was "on the road again," but this time it was for a far better purpose than it ever had been when I was driving the truck.

The drudgery of driving in order to make a living had been replaced with a sense of wonder, excitement, expectancy, and joy. Every waking thought was mixed with anticipation: "I wonder what God has in store for me?"

Along familiar interstates that led through the Great Plains, across the mighty Mississippi, over the hills and farmlands of the north central states, I kept driving eastward. God's purpose was my goal.

At tollbooths and turnstiles, in restaurants and motels along the way, I told people about Jesus. Their response amazed me. No one was offended. Most were open. Some had tears in their eyes as I shared the Gospel with them. It was as if a select few had been waiting to hear the good news I had shared with them. Some even gave their hearts to Jesus as I escorted them into God's Kingdom. Grandmother's prophecy had come true; I was a priest leading the people to God. I was like the mendicant friars of the Middle Ages, spreading the seeds of the Gospel everywhere I went.

Though my ultimate destination (except for heaven) was still unknown to me. I felt strongly impelled to go to the town where my first wife and many of my children lived. Near the Blue Ridge Mountains of North Carolina, the little town of Morgantown is situated in the rolling foothills of the Piedmont Region.

I spent two wonderful months in Morgantown with Viola and my children. My ex-wife and the kids noticed the change in me almost immediately. Surely, this is where God wants me, I continued to hope.

Some months previously, I had sent a gift Bible to Viola. She had expressed her appreciation for it, and forgave me when I confessed to her my many failings as her husband. Though the time we spent together was very meaningful, God still had other plans for me, and I was ready to follow Him.

Roots in the Sandy Loam

Could New Jersey—my home state—be my Nineveh? I felt backed against a wall. Was I like Jonah, trying to avoid God's clear call to go to the place of His choice, to preach? North Carolina was so beautiful. I took a stroll into the woods to spend time with the Lord one day, when I was made aware of one of nature's sounds. When I looked up, I noticed it was an owl hooting and circling overhead in broad daylight. Squirrels scampered up and down trees and circled around my feet. These animals, normally afraid of humans, played all around me as I prayed in the spirit. Then I understood that the peace of God would be in New Jersey, and no matter where God would lead me, I would experience His peace in the same way that there was no fear in the wild animals. Fortunately, I did not have to spend time in the belly of a whale in order to discover His will!

I left North Carolina behind and headed north to the state where my roots are—to the sandy loam of New Jersey—a state that is rich in its variety of people, terrain, and activities. People from every ethnic background live and work in New Jersey. It is a state that is known for its tomatoes, asparagus, Italian food, pizzerias, diners, gambling casinos, beaches, pine barrens, mountains, rivers, lakes, farmland, industrial centers, airports, marshes, parkways, expressways, turnpikes, bridges, pollution, housing developments, and Revolutionary War history.

When some people think of New Jersey, they envision the factories surrounding the Meadowlands near Newark International Airport. Others think of the race riots that took place after Marin Luther King's assassination in 1968. Still others think of the George Washington Bridge, of Giants'

Stadium, the Walt Whitman Bridge, Camden, Cape May, and Wildwood-by-the-Sea. Some think of Atlantic City— the Vegas of the East—a glitzy casino town with a once-famous boardwalk that was known for its Steel Pier and diving horses. It is the home of the annual Miss America Pageant, and the setting for the board game called Monopoly.

Folks will often ask me, "How did New Jersey come to be called 'the Garden State'?" They have never seen the multitudinous acres of farmland in the southern part of the state or the horse farms of central New Jersey.

Many people, including Christians, fail to realize that a spiritual revival is taking place in my home state. Our churches are growing, and the word of faith is spreading. Exciting things are taking place in the Garden State.

When I became a Christian, New Jersey seemed like a dark place in my past. I viewed it as a place where sin and sorrow reigned. It was the environment in which I had spent my first fifty years in sin and degradation. I served the lord of my own selfish desires in my earlier life in New Jersey, and I remembered many of the painful mistakes I had made there. These are the reasons why it was a real struggle for me to return there.

God had made it abundantly clear to me, however, that He wanted me to return to the place where my roots had been planted fifty-some years ago. He literally commanded me, *Vinny, go to New Jersey.* I knew I had no option but to obey, but I hoped He only wanted me to stay there a brief while.

Painful memories mixed with some nostalgia as I drove over the Delaware Memorial Bridge into Salem County, New Jersey. The belching smoke stacks of refineries and chemical companies along the river greeted me with their unpleasant stench and gray clouds. The darkness of their pollution reminded me of my first fifty years of darkness.

By the time I entered the New Jersey Turnpike, however, the gloomy feelings were replaced with a rippling excitement that began to course through my being. I responded with prayer, "Heavenly Father, thank you for the good time I had with my family in North Carolina. I feel certain that you helped me to take care of some unfinished business with Viola and the kids. Thank you for their openness, Lord. Bless their lives with an intimate personal knowledge of you. Lead each one to a saving knowledge of Jesus Christ and help me to always be a faithful witness to them."

Tractor-trailers roared past me on the highway as I headed north beyond exit two, the Swedesboro exit on the turnpike. At about that moment, my mind's eye captured a vivid picture of the accident Rocco and I had experienced in Bay City, Michigan, several years before. "God, thank you for saving my life that day," I prayed. "I know you did so for a purpose, and now I am beginning to see that purpose more clearly. I realize that you want me to reach people with the saving knowledge of your love. You sent your Son for everyone, and it will be my privilege to tell all you lead me to about Jesus. Continue to reveal your plan and purpose to me."

Peace and joy flooded my soul. The clouds disappeared. In that single instant, all the gloom and reservations I had associated with a return to New Jersey began to vanish. God had exchanged the negative feelings with an excited sense of purpose. Inwardly, however, I still hoped God would lead me somewhere other than New Jersey, and I wanted my sojourn there to be brief.

My brother Phil lived in Woodbridge, not far from exit 9 on the New Jersey Turnpike. His home was my first stop. I

31

told Phil about my experience with Jesus, and he remarked, "Vinny, I can certainly see a tremendous change in your life." He recommended that I pay my brother Richard a visit in nearby Connecticut.

Before long, I drove to Connecticut in order to share the Gospel with my brother Richard. Though he listened intently and respectfully, he did not accept Jesus then and there. We enjoyed several hours of reminiscing together, and after a couple of days, I felt impelled to return to my native New Jersey.

As I drove back south across the George Washington Bridge, I felt as if God was sitting in the passenger seat with me. He and I kept a dialogue going for hours. He reminded me of an old friend named Lou who was in the trucking business in northern New Jersey. He had once been controller for Longo Trucking, and I knew he would welcome me as he had done with so many others. I had helped Lou get started in the trucking industry many years before.

He lived in Manolopen, New Jersey, where he raised race horses. His trucking firm was in South Plainfield, not far from Interstate 287.

"It's nice to see you again, Vinny, " he greeted. "Welcome to my humble abode."

Far from being humble, Lou's home was truly palatial. His hard work had proven to be very profitable for him and his family, and I was happy to see him in such a successful situation.

The two of us chatted for a while, and then Lou remarked, " You look the same, Vinny, but you sound different." We laughed together and I realized my words were reaching his heart.

The next morning Lou invited me to stay with him and to work for him in either the trucking company or with the race horses. I told him I didn't know anything about race horses, but I thought I knew something about trucks, and so I accepted his offer with gratitude while still hoping that New Jersey and this job were temporary changes in my life.

The Devil Made It Clear!

Amazingly, I found myself working with trucks again! Lou's terminal in South Plainfield is located at the end of a rather isolated, wooded stretch of road. It is a dead end street that is called Hollywood Avenue. In the light of what happened there soon after my work with Lou began, I think the street's name is very appropriate!

One morning I took one of his trucks to Route 1 in Edison. Along the way I needed to stop at the Mack Company in order to pick up some parts.

I hardly ever ate breakfast in those days. Therefore, I was surprised when the Lord clearly directed me, *Vinny, I want you to stop at the diner and eat breakfast.* This was very unusual, but the urge was so strong that I felt compelled to obey.

I went into the diner and ordered fried eggs, bacon, and coffee. It was a fantastic breakfast, but I kept wondering about God's direction as I ate. Is there someone here that He wants me to witness to? The waitresses were so busy that I couldn't strike up a conversation with them, and the men next to me at the counter were reading the newspaper. What did it all mean?

I soon understood the Lord's direction. As I was returning to work several minutes later, right after turning onto Hollywood Avenue, I saw red lights, police vehicles, and swarms of people milling about in front of the terminal at the end of the lane. As I got closer, I saw police dogs, cruisers, shotguns, and plain-clothes detectives surrounding the area.

One of our mechanics rushed up to meet me. "You missed all the fun, Vinny," he announced as he approached my cab.

"What happened here?"

"Well, I'm not sure you want to know," he continued. "You really didn't miss any fun at all. As a matter of fact, you may have missed your own murder!"

"My own murder!?"

"Yes, you know what happened? Somebody came out of the woods over there, and began shooting at the truck you were working on. If you had been here, you would have been killed!"

"No way! You mean . . ."

"I'm telling you, Vinny, they emptied a 45-calibre handgun at the truck. Thank God you weren't here. You would surely have been murdered!"

I saw where the bullets had glazed off the truck at the very spot where I would have been standing.

"But why would somebody do such a thing?"

"We don't have any idea. The police are looking for the culprits. Is there somebody out to get you?"

" Just the devil," I said. "Just the devil."

The mechanic shook his head as if he was confused and then said, "Well, thank God, the devil is such a poor shot."

As I stepped out of the cab, my heart soared with gratitude to the Father who had protected me by giving me the direction to eat breakfast at the diner. Not only did I get a good meal, but I was still alive! Had I returned to the terminal at the regular time, I would have been killed. "Thank you, Father. Thank you."

Briefly I was reminded of my earthly father who had protected me in the moments after my birth by demanding to see me. Had he not intervened I would have been born dead! Now, however, I had been born again. The devil saw God's pure gold inside of me and he wanted it. My heavenly Father protected me. I continued my prayer, "Thank you Father. Thank you for keeping me alive so I could accomplish your purposes."

God, in His foreknowledge, had seen what was going to take place at the terminal, and He protected me. The devil was out to destroy me, but he failed because the Lord is ever-more-powerful than he is.

Not long afterward, the police apprehended the Satan-led criminals who served as his pawns, even though they were so drug-crazed that they had no idea of what they had done. There was no rhyme or reason for their shooting at the truck, except for the fact that they were so strung out on drugs that the devil was able to use them against me. They didn't even know where they were. They had driven south on the interstate from northern New Jersey and had "just happened" to turn off onto a dirt road in the woods near the terminal.

Of all the byways and cul-de-sacs, highways, streets, roads, and lanes they could have chosen, why did they select the area near Hollywood Avenue? I knew the answer. The devil did not want me in New Jersey!

Now I knew for certain that New Jersey was the place for me. This event had made it completely clear to me. "Lord, I will stay here, and obey you. Where you lead me I will follow."

That afternoon I heard His now-familiar voice, *Patience, Vinny, patience.*

A Special Surprise

It had never occurred to me that a new marriage would be part of God's plan for me. I knew He was preparing me for ministry, but marriage seemed to be only a remote possibility. I felt I had failed in two marriages already, and I was not really eager to try again. God had promised a ministry to me, and that was my goal. At the same time, however, there were times of loneliness and I was well-aware of God's admonition, "It is not good that the man should be alone, I will make him an help meet for him" (Gen. 2:18).

My brother Phil had become a Christian, and he told me about a unique church he was attending in Plainfield, New Jersey.

I found the church in a quiet residential area. Stately Victorian homes bordered by gigantic azalea bushes gave the neighborhood a very clean and prosperous appearance. The church itself was relatively plain, however, and it was joined to a large Victorian home that served as a facility for offices, meetings, and classrooms. The church had acquired several properties in the vicinity, including a beautiful apartment building next door.

The first thing I noticed as I walked through the front door of the church were the golden letters forming the name of Jesus arching over the altar in front of the sanctuary. What a great place this must be, I reflected. Jesus is their focal point; He is the center of their lives and worship; everything that happens here takes place under His name! Next, I was impressed with the variety of the people who worshiped there. The church was full, and under the name of Jesus people of all backgrounds worshiped and fellowshipped together. Rich and poor, black and white, old and young, Catholic, Jewish, and Protestant—a cross section of humanity gathering under the name of Jesus and showing amazing love and acceptance for one another. I loved it! The atmosphere was electrified with the power of the Holy Spirit!

I began to attend services there on a regular basis. The pastor, Bob McCaffrey, was a loving man who obviously enjoyed teaching the truths of God's Word. He was an excellent teacher, and the atmosphere of praise and worship seemed truly heavenly.

As I mentioned before, I was greatly impressed with the love the people expressed for one another. They readily accepted me and I loved them. We prayed together, studied God's Word together, and had memorable times of fellowship at local diners and pizzerias. These people loved Jesus, and it was a joy to worship with them.

One Sunday, as I was preparing to sit down after an especially meaningful time of worship, my attention was strangely drawn to the back of a lady's head. She was sitting about three pews ahead of me on the same side of the sanctuary. Her lovely auburn hair seemed to glow with a brilliant radiance that caught me off-guard. The shine of her hair seemed to possess a supernatural quality.

God said, *Vinny, I want you to pray for her. Bless her.*

For a moment I wondered why He had directed me to pray for this unknown lady.

That's your wife! He gently announced.

I was stunned. This was not the answer I was expecting. I thought He might have wanted me to pray for her health, her finances, her family, or some other need.

"What did you say?" I questioned.

Vinny, she's your wife!

Twice He had given me the same message. "My wife!?"

Yes, your wife, He repeated.

This was the third time He told me, and now the answer was beginning to intrigue me. God was beginning to prepare me for marriage to a woman I had never met. A woman with beautiful auburn hair! The thought hit me, " But I've never even seen her face!"

I closed my eyes and prayed for her. When I was finished, I glanced up and at precisely that same moment, the mysterious lady (who was to be my wife) turned around and looked directly at me!

The same glow that surrounded her hair emanated from her pretty face. Her sparkling eyes told me that this woman was deeply interested in spiritual things. I gave her one of my sweetest Italian smiles as our eyes met, and we locked our gaze upon each other's eyes. What passed between us in those few moments was complete attraction—it was both spiritual and physical, and it was truly exciting. This lady was a special surprise for me—a totally unexpected blessing from the hands of my heavenly Father. I loved her immediately. I wanted to get to know her. In fact, I was drawn to her.

After the service I asked a friend who was sitting nearby if he knew the lady with the auburn hair. I learned that her name was Nancy, a single mother who worked as a manicurist and had recently begun attending services at this church.

I had never had a manicure and felt that real men never should have them, but I was determined to get to know this beautiful woman, even if it meant having to get a manicure! Phil told me he knew exactly where she worked.

The next day I went to the beauty parlor and introduced myself to the beautiful Nancy who had been occupying all my waking dreams. "Hi, Nancy, my name is Vinny. I saw you last Sunday in church, and I've been praying for you ever since. Remember me?"

"Yes, I do remember you," she remarked. "God told me to turn around that day and pray for you. At first I thought I was supposed to pray for Phil, but then I noticed you standing there, holding your Bible and looking very much like a prophet!"

We laughed a great deal that morning as we chatted for a few moments. I invited Nancy to go out with me and she agreed. My heart soared with joy!

I learned that my future wife was a new Christian who wanted very much to please the Lord in every area of her life.

She truly was a handmaiden of the Lord - an ideal kind of helpmate for a man who would be in the ministry. I was intrigued by her sweet spirit.

We prayed together on our first date. God had begun our relationship by asking us to pray for each other, and prayer became the theme of our relationship. Through times of prayer together, and alone, we got to know each other's hearts. It was wonderful.

Over pizza and Pepsi one night, Nancy told me about some of her struggles. Life had dealt her some hard blows. Her seventeen-year-old-son had been using drugs since he was twelve. She was learning how to cast her cares upon the Lord, and God was meeting her needs in miraculous ways. A former Roman Catholic, Nancy still struggled with confusion stemming from her religious traditions. I could certainly identify with her in this area.

She told me, "When I first saw you, Vinny, it seemed as if there was a glow around you. You seemed so strong in the Lord, standing there, clutching your Bible, and I immediately was impressed with a sense of spiritual authority that emanated from you. You are like a general in the Lord's army."

We shared so many interests and values. We like to do the same kind of things. We even enjoyed the same kinds of foods. Soon, we started attending church together.

In one service Pastor McCaffrey gave an altar call for release from bondages. I wondered why Nancy was standing up for prayer. As I looked up at her, I saw a vision of a halo over her head. God directed me, *Vinny, go and break her of that bondage.*

I was not certain yet as to what "that bondage" was, but I obeyed the Lord. When I laid my hands on Nancy's head, she fell under the power of God's Spirit. A mighty deliverance

39

was taking place, and soon I realized that it was a release from her bondage to Catholic religious traditions. She had been praying to the saints for many years, and God wanted her to realize that she could address her prayers directly to Him.

Jesus' mother, Mary, is to be honored as the mother of our Savior, but she is not to be worshiped as the mother of God. The saints who are revered in the Roman Catholic church have accomplished many wonderful things for God, but it is unscriptural to pray to them. St. Paul makes this abundantly clear: "For there is one God, and one mediator between God and men, the man Christ Jesus" (1 Tim. 2:5).

When Nancy went back to her home that evening she decided to remove the 100-pound statue of Mary that occupied a corner of her living room where there was a makeshift altar with candles, statues, and other religious material. God was setting Nancy free.

Our relationship grew and grew. We prayed together, sang choruses in the car, attended church together, and talked about Jesus continuously. Our relationship was squarely based upon the Bible, and even when we went to the Jersey Shore, we would sit on the beach and read God's Word. It was a wonderful time of courtship, friendship, and fellowship.

Eventually, we started to minister together as well. God was getting us ready for the fulfillment of His call on our lives.

Our Father showed us that we are children of light. The supernatural radiance that attracted us to each other in the first place is the light of His Spirit reflecting from us.

We soon discovered that other people are attracted to the light of God that emanates from us. People are always drawn to the light of God. As a matter of fact, when we notice someone staring at us in a restaurant, on the boardwalk, in a public place, we believe that it is someone who is being attracted to the light of God. We want our light to always shine in the darkness. God commands us to keep our light shining before men.

One day as we were having lunch in a diner on Route 1, we noticed a frail elderly lady who was watching us intently. God said, *Pray for her. She has cancer.*

Soon afterward she walked over to our table and I said, "You have a sickness, and Jesus wants to heal you."

"Yes, I have cancer, " she acknowledged. " But I am Jewish."

"Jesus loves you, ma'am," I pointed out. "He was Jewish, and He loves the Jewish people. We love you too." We prayed with her briefly while her husband was paying their bill at the register. He appeared to be annoyed by what he obviously regarded as our intrusion into their affairs, but the lady's countenance brightened so much as we prayed for her healing. We are confident that God heard our prayers for her, as well as the cries of her heart, even though her husband interrupted with a gruff roar, " Get over here!"

From that day to this, Nancy and I have been involved in the exciting adventure of being led by God's Spirit in ministry. He leads us to the people who really need His love. It's always wonderful to see a new Christian blossom like a spring flower in the sunshine of God's love.

Nancy and I were meant for each other. Our marriage is a partnership in ministry. On Thanksgiving Day, 1982, we were joined in Holy Matrimony. We both knew we had heard from God about each other, and in a beautiful moonlight service we exchanged our vows to each other and to the One who brought us together. Indeed, it was a Thanksgiving Day on which we had so much to thank God for. Each day since then has been a Thanksgiving Day, as Nancy and I serve our King together.

3

A Fulfilling Promise

Through many dangers, toils, and snares
I have already come,
'Tis grace hath brought me safe thus far,
And grace will lead me home.

(John Newton)

Each for the Other—Both for the Lord

The Lord uses the metaphor of marriage to typify his relationship with His bride—the Church. The elements of faithfulness, trust, and commitment are required in both relationships.

My marriage to Nancy helped me to see so many spiritual truths more clearly. I truly recognize her to be God's gift of grace to me. Nancy provides me with the balance I need to walk harmoniously with the Lord and with my fellowman.

Soon after her deliverance from idolatry, Nancy became a bold witness for the Lord Jesus Christ. She shared the Gospel with everyone without fear or reservation. She amazed me as I watched her lead soul after soul into the Kingdom of God.

Our marriage began in the soil of Christian love and commitment. It was the only time I had begun a marriage in this way. In contrast with the way my other marriages had begun and developed, I understood why so many marriages end in divorce. Without the Lord at the center of the home, the family drifts on a sea of selfishness and confusion. The wonder is not that so many marriages break apart, but rather that so many marriages (without Christ) remain intact!

Our relationship has been watered with the Word of God and nurtured by the sunshine of His continuous love. We are growing in God together. Truly, we have learned how to flow together in ministry to others and to each other. Oftentimes, God inspires both of us with the need to minister to someone at precisely the same moment.

Nancy and I begin each day and close each day with prayer. This enables us to remain sensitive to the Lord and to each other. It also enables us to keep the lines of communication open and to receive God's direction for our marriage and our ministry.

Nancy is a humble handmaiden of the Lord who was hand-picked by the Father to be my bride. Ours was, therefore, an arranged marriage. Not arranged by our earthly parents, to be sure, but arranged by our Father in heaven. My love for my bride grows stronger with each passing day. To be yoked together with such a sincere Christian lady gives me the grace to always strive to love her as Christ loves His Church.

"Husbands, love your wives, even as Christ also loved the church, and gave himself for it; That he might sanctify and cleanse it with the washing of the water by the word" (Eph. 5:

25-26). The extended analogy Paul gives us in Ephesians 5 is the ideal marriage, and Nancy and I strive each day to follow this pattern in our relationship.

This is not to say, however, that we never have disagreements. Actually the disagreements help us to see more clearly our need for God's wisdom and for each other. In the disagreements we look for God's hand at work, and we turn to Him for the answers we seek. He has already supplied us with the resources and tools we need to resolve all conflicts through prayer, Bible study, and open communication.

I recognize my role as the priest in our home, and Nancy respects me in that role. As her priest, it is my responsibility to pray for her (and all my family), to love them, teach them, guide them, and bless them. What an honor and privilege it is for me to do so.

Nancy honors me in the way outlined by Paul: "Wives, submit yourselves unto your own husbands, as unto the Lord" (Eph. 5:22). She defers to me in areas involving spiritual decisions, fully trusting that God will reveal His will through me. When she feels that I have made a mistake, she will tell me so in a loving way, and most of the time, after I think the issue through, I discover she was right! So many times Nancy has had spiritual insights that far exceed my own.

When this happens, I confess my mistakes to God and to her, and then I pursue another alternative which seems to be more in line with God's will. In many ways, our marriage has become one of mutual submission—each for the other and both for the Lord. That is what Paul implies in Ephesians 5: "Wherefore be ye not unwise, but understanding what the will of the Lord is . . . Submitting yourselves one to another in the fear of God" (Eph 5:18, 21).

The ideal for Christian marriage is clear, but it cannot work if only one partner is investing personal energy into the relationship. It requires both partners giving 100%. The husband must love his wife as Christ loves the Church— forgiving her, protecting her, and laying down his life for her. The wife must reverence her husband as she does the Lord. My precious Nancy constantly fosters the spiritual environment we need in our home.

Faith Fellowship

Nancy and I began attending Christian concerts that were presented in the facilities of a Christian bookstore on Route 1 in Edison, New Jersey. The store, owned by Carl Teschke and Joe Catalano, is called Jesus Book and Gift Store. It is located on a busy thoroughfare, along a stretch of highway that leads from the Philadelphia area to New York City. Along the way one notices restaurants like Bennigan's, Exxon stations, factories of various sorts, an adult bookstore, diners, and motels. It is a congested area where the name of Jesus stands in stark contrast with the world of materialistic darkness.

Richie Gomez and his band had often presented concerts there. I soon learned that Richie and some others had plans to become part of a new church starting up in nearby Iselin, New Jersey. The church would be meeting in a former synagogue on Cooper Avenue in Iselin, an area that I was not familiar with. They were relocating there from Staten Island, New York.

After talking and praying with Nancy, I felt an inner desire to seek out this new church. We had learned that its name would be Faith Fellowship. I wanted to meet the church's pastor, a man I had already heard many good things about. So one day, after dropping Nancy off at work, I drove to the Iselin area in an effort to find the former synagogue on Cooper Avenue. First, of course, I had to find Cooper Avenue, and that was no easy task in itself! A kind gentleman who was walking his St. Bernard along a street with shops and businesses directed me to Cooper Avenue, but he had no idea where the synagogue was located.

I drove along the tree-lined street for several minutes, then I turned around. On my second pass I noticed some men unloading a van in front of a rather unimpressive, plain building with a stucco exterior. "Do you know where Faith Fellowship is?" I inquired.

"You're in front of it," one smiling young man in jeans declared as he pointed to the building I just described. "Come in, I'll introduce you to our pastor."

We walked into the little building and I noticed a man running a buffer over the floors of the hallway. "This is Pastor DeMola," the youth said. "Pastor, this man has been looking for our church."

"Welcome to Faith Fellowship," the man who was running the buffer greeted. He looked more like a janitor than a pastor, but his sparkling eyes and his brilliant smile told me that this man knew Jesus. He was Pastor David DeMola, a man with a winsome, vibrant sense of humor, and a great love for people. He held out his hand and asked my name.

"I'm Vinny Longo and I've been hearing about your church from people at the Jesus Book and Gift Store. I was hoping to be able to meet you and learn about your church."

"Certainly, Vinny. We're glad you've come."

There was something very extraordinary about this man. I learned a lot about him from his strong handshake, his personal warmth, and his caring response. My years in business had taught me to look for such things in attempting

47

to judge the character of a person, and immediately I knew I was in the presence of a true man of God who possessed uncommon strength of character.

He took me into the room that would eventually serve as his study and he spent some time with me. I greatly appreciated the personal attention he gave to me. He spoke about his hopes and goals for Faith Fellowship. At the end of our meeting he urged, "Come back and see us again, Vinny."

The time spent with Pastor DeMola caused me to know that Faith Fellowship would become our church home. Their emphasis on the Word of God—and the faith it imparts to the human heart—was so important to me. I knew that faith is developed by hearing the Word of God (See Rom 10:17). I also knew that without faith it is impossible to please God (See Heb. 11:6). I wanted to grow in faith, and I wanted to please God. For these reasons I knew that Faith Fellowship was for us.

Before long, Nancy and I said good-bye to our many good friends at the church in Plainfield and we joined Faith Fellowship. It was hard to say good-bye to the fellow-believers who had been so much a part of our lives while we were growing in the Lord. These were the people who had supported us spiritually and encouraged us as we were planning to marry. They are wonderful people of God.

Faith Fellowship grew very quickly. It began with approximately seventy members, some of whom were coming from Staten Island, but before long, the fellowship of believers outgrew the small synagogue.

By 1985, the congregation was able to build a new, much larger church building on Oaktree Road in Edison, New Jersey, under the dynamic leadership of Pastor DeMola. It was a vital community of faith—loving people reaching out to the spiritually starved folks of that congested section of central

New Jersey. No other church in the area was providing such a powerful witness in that area. The pastor's teaching ministry was enabling many to find freedom; he was ministering to individuals and families from a wide range of backgrounds. His message was always strong in faith, and under his ministry, Nancy and I experienced phenomenal spiritual growth and change. I remember thinking, "If only I had known these things thirty years ago!"

God was preparing us for a ministry that would one day exceed all our expectations. He was fulfilling a dream, a prophecy, a promise He had given to us. It was as if I had exchanged my citizenship from America and this earth to citizenship in heaven. I felt as if I was a stranger who was sojourning in a foreign land. I saw all of life differently.

Faith Is the Victory

An usher in the church came to me one morning and said, "You know, Vinny, as I was praying, the Lord told me to tell you we need to have Victory in Jesus meetings in our church to present this vision to you and to ask you to be my co-worker."

The usher's name was John, and I had enjoyed wonderful fellowship with him over the first few months at Faith Fellowship. "What's that, John?" I wondered aloud.

"Well, in my former church we had a special ministry to drug addicts and alcoholics, and we called it Victory in Jesus fellowship. Don't you think we need something like that here?"

I thought for a brief moment. I was certainly aware of the problems in our area—and even in some families of the church—but I never had a drawing to that kind of ministry. I knew that John must be thinking that he and I should start such a program, but I wasn't sure about it. Our over-populated area was rife with problems related to drugs, including violence, crime, AIDS, and I knew the public schools were grappling with these issues every day.

"Yes, John, there certainly is a need," I agreed.

He had to get back to ushering, but John's suggestion replayed in my mind throughout the worship service. My head was in conflict with my heart. I reflected, "Yes, there is a need, but that kind of ministry is very difficult."

The focus of my ministry was on teaching and evangelism. I loved to do both. It was thrilling for me to lead a soul to Jesus Christ and to teach that person the truths of the Gospel. I yearned to be able to get involved with the discipling of new converts. Jesus had completely transformed my life, and I knew without any reservation, beyond all doubt, that He was the answer, no matter what the question. My heart's desire was to be in deep spiritual ministry to people.

My mind continued to reflect on John's idea as the service progressed. When the time of dedication and worship arrived, I stood to my feet and told the Lord, "Though the Victory in Jesus idea is not as glamorous as the ministry I had envisioned, Father, I submit this possibility to you, and I ask you to show me if I should join with John in starting this outreach at our church. Father, I want only to do your will, no matter what it is. If it is your desire for me to just stay on as a prayer-room worker that's what I'll do, but I firmly believe that you have put this desire for ministry in my heart and I know you will bring it to fruition. Lord, is Victory in Jesus the ministry for me?"

The answer was unequivocal: *Vinny, this is the ministry I have chosen for you.*

That was all I needed to hear. After the service, I shared this exciting news with Nancy. She seemed overjoyed by the prospect of working together with me in such a context, although a bit overwhelmed by the subject matter.

Then I got back with John. Within moments, the two of us had set our ministry goal.

"We'll need to submit this to Pastor," I suggested.

"Yes, of course," he acknowledged, "Let's see if we can schedule an appointment with him."

The thrill of anticipation flooded my being throughout that week as I prayed about it, talked about it with Nancy and John, and thought about it. It would be a wonderful way to blend together the gifts God had imparted to me in ministry. I could not wait to present the plan to our pastor.

Later that week, John and I met with Pastor DeMola, who gave us full encouragement. "Yes, such a ministry will help our fellowship in many important ways. You can have rooms to meet in."

We were launched! Victory in Jesus held its first meeting the next Tuesday. Though it was sparsely attended, we sensed that God was there with us. We could feel the warmth of His smile as we ministered in His name. That experience taught me many things, including never to despise the "day of small beginnings."

Little Is Much When God Is in It

God was with us each step of the way. His hand was directing us, and we knew with clarity that Victory in Jesus was within His perfect will. That first meeting that I alluded to earlier was attended by John, Nancy, another church member, and a lady who was dealing with her alcoholic brother.

We counseled with the lady by sharing God's Word with her. "Martha, the Word of God says, 'If two of you shall agree on earth as touching any thing that they shall ask, it shall be done for them of my Father which is in heaven. For where two or three are gathered together in my name, there am I in the midst of them' (Matt. 18:19-20). Let's pray."

Martha and John and I joined hands as I prayed, "Spirit of alcoholism, we bind you in Jesus' name and we command you to loose Walter."

Then we prayed, "Father, Martha is your covenant child and she's come here to stand in the gap for her brother, Walter. So we lift him up to you and ask you to draw him to you, Lord. Open up the eyes of his spiritual understanding and draw him into your borders, so that he can come to know you as we do. We give you thanks and praise and glory for all you're about to do in his life. We ask it in Jesus' precious name. Amen."

We knew the answer had been accomplished in the spiritual realm. We had petitioned God for favor on Martha's brother, and we believed there would be a change in his life that would be made, not by human hands. We sensed that it was only a matter of time before we would hear some good news about Walter. I knew it, and John knew it, but Martha didn't. She still needed teaching, so I encouraged her by saying, "Martha, alcoholism is not a sickness, as many have suggested; it's a symptom, a reflection of a spiritual problem."

She nodded as I continued, "Spiritual problems have to be confronted with spiritual solutions. If a person does not know Jesus Christ as his Savior, he has no real ability to control the situations of his life. No matter how many things he turns to, to help support his needs, he'll always be lacking the ability to change, because all changes take place in the spiritual realm first and then it shows up in the physical (natural) realm."

"But how can I get through to him? I believe what you are telling me."

"When we pray, we have to believe we are effecting those changes as we battle in the spirit-realm, and it's vital that you keep growing in the Lord, because knowledge about Him will sharpen your prayers. When we prayed, just now, we interceded for your brother, and we got in the middle of the situation before God and we asked Him for a blessing on Walter. Remember, the enemy's goal for your brother is destruction, so buttress yourself against the powers of darkness and become the wall where destruction must stop. Begin to envision your brother as a child of God instead of an alcoholic, one who is free to praise and glorify Him, and the Lord will take care of His part. God is faithful; He never changes. No matter what happens, don't give up until you see the victory, because it's done. Expect good news."

Some months later we learned that Walter had stopped drinking, he had been set free, and had begun that wonderful journey of walking in the light of God's Word.

That first meeting of Victory in Jesus was conducted on December 3, 1985, and we have been meeting ever since that time. Through this outreach God is fulfilling His promise to me and Nancy. As our little ministry has grown, God has proven himself to be ever-faithful. He knows what we need even before we present the need to Him. He is our awesome and mighty God!

We continually seek the Lord for clear direction with regard to the focus of our ministry. In those early days, God spoke to my heart by saying, *Vinny, preach the Word by faith.* And that's what Nancy and I have been doing ever since.

The Battle Begins

We have worked with countless individuals who struggle with a variety of dependencies. Some come for themselves, others for a dear family member. Most of them, however, have no idea how or why they became enslaved to a chemical, a behavior, a person, or a habit. They don't realize that they have been deceived by the enemy of their souls who is out to destroy them. All they know, in most cases, is that they are subject (in bondage) to something that seems to be completely hopeless. Indeed, their very lives are out of control!

Many who have come to us have literally been at death's door, and we are able to help them find hope in the midst of their hopelessness. Some feel so hopeless that they've become suicidal. Taking their own lives has become their only apparent option.

Society's stereotype of the drug addict was blown to smithereens as businessmen, secretaries, clergy, lawyers, teachers, bankers, doctors, and housewives came for help along with street people, former criminals, teen-agers, and gang members. Satan's schemes had ensnared them without respect to their social status, economic position, education, religious training, age, or occupation. Once enslaved, they felt hopelessly imprisoned. For those who didn't know the Lord, an addictive life-style was the only inheritance the world had to offer them, but our biggest, long and drawn-out battles, we would discover soon, would be fought for the saints, born-again Christians who had long been held captive. Born again, but still slaves of the flesh. God had given us the job of helping to free them.

We soon realized, without formal training in social work or psychology, that bondages are the fruit of the enemy. When a person does not know God, something other than the one, true God will become the ruler of that life. They live in the kingdom of darkness. The person's weakness will be used by the enemy against him, whether that weakness be a person, a drug, or a behavior. As the lost try to fix the emptiness that cries to be filled deep within their spirits, they are deceived into thinking that fleeting pleasures (temporary highs) are the answers to their sense of hopelessness and emptiness, but their spirits have a vacant spot that can only be filled with God.

Their addictions soon set a downward spiral in motion, and they sense that the emptiness remains empty, the hopelessness remains hopeless, and they are bereft of friends, meaning, goals, and other resources. Loneliness and a sense of isolation are inevitable ingredients of addictions as well, and frequently the addicted one loses touch with reality, his feelings, God, his relationships, and even himself. Such a person is truly alone.

Dependencies block one's creativity, ability to love, feelings, dreams, and aspirations, and that's exactly what the enemy wants. Numbed by their addictions, many are unable to hold onto significant relationships in their lives, and as a result, they often sustain further losses in all areas of their lives—financially, occupationally, relationally, etc.

Any loss causes mourning and grief, and because the captive has endured so many losses, he has been perfectly set up by the enemy for further attacks, such as depression and aimlessness. This is the case with many who come to Victory in Jesus meetings. They are literally sloshing around in Bunyan's "slough of despond." Like the Prodigal Son in Jesus' parable, they have dissipated their rightful inheritance with sinful pursuits and are now lost and need to be found. Born-again Christians, finding themselves in this position, either lack the knowledge of God they need to fight for victory or they don't even realize they have an enemy.

Many who come to our meetings the first time do so because concerned friends or family members have invited them or encouraged them to do so. They do not come on their own initiative. One alcoholic who had gone through several twelve-step programs with little success did come to our meeting on his own initiative. He wanted answers. He wanted to get free.

This struggling man was a Wall Street broker who admitted to me," Vinny, I always thought that I was a self-sufficient man who could lick any problem that came my way. I used alcohol to nurse my inner hurts, but eventually the beloved bottle took control of my life. I began to live for nothing but my next drink."

I remembered what I used to be like. Though alcohol was not my particular addiction, I could relate to the bondage he described. Like him, my own sense of self-sufficiency, my pride, had been my idol. God had been far removed from my life. My life had once been out of control, and this is what welled up the compassion of God within me for him. This is what made me know that this gentleman's answer was the same as it had been for me—it was Jesus—for only Jesus can meet the deep needs of the human heart.

It was my privilege to be able to lead this man to a saving knowledge of Jesus Christ by showing him that I did understand what it had been like for him. I knew what his struggle was like because I had been there. God is no respecter of persons. What He had done for me He would do for him. All it required was a heart that was submissive to the Lordship of Christ.

A Change in Perspective

Eventually Victory in Jesus grew to such an extent that we had to add staff members who could help us with the ministry. The Friday evening meetings had changed from a small-group format to large meetings that resembled worship services. Ten people gave of their time and talents to the music ministry of our outreach, and we were so grateful for their help in leading us into the pleasures of worship.

John, Nancy, and I worked in unbroken harmony for three years. God gave us a spirit of unity and joy as we ministered together, prayed together, and dreamed together. Our calling was clear, and we kept our focus sharply pointed on our ministry to the "down-and-outers" and the " up-and-outers." The full leadership of Victory in Jesus fell into the hands of Nancy and me after our good friend John unexpectedly withdrew due to other demands that required his attention. We missed John greatly because he was so much a part of us and the ministry, but God had other plans for him, and Nancy and I blessed him as he went forth to a different field of service.

We had seen glorious victories in those first three years. People were healed of terminal illnesses as well as inner hurts. Former homosexuals had been set free from their bondages to the flesh. Marriages had been restored. Alcoholics and drug addicts had found lasting sobriety. AIDS patients grew stronger. But there were struggles along the way as well. There were defeats. There were failures.

One day the Lord instructed me by saying, *Vinny, these people have to understand there are two sides to every life—the spiritual (where the problem really is) and the natural side (where the problem is manifested). Your job is to show them how their problem begins—and how it manifests in the natural side.*

The Lord then led me to Romans 7 and 8 where Paul discusses the conflict between the spiritual and natural sides of our lives. He states, "For I know that in me (that is, in my flesh,) dwelleth no good thing, but how to perform that which is good I find not. For the good that I would, I do not: but the evil which I would not, that I do" (Rom 7:18-19).

57

No good thing dwells in our flesh—nothing good at all. Our fleshly ability to reason cannot win any battle. Neither can our fleshly zeal. The power of the human will, even, is weak when it comes to a truly spiritual battle, because the will does not operate on its own. The will of a man receives direction from the spiritual realm, and that direction is either divine or satanic.

God clearly showed me that the battle is against spiritual bondage. I had to teach people how to battle in the spiritual realm in order to win. If I could get them to see into the spirit-realm, they would see their position in it. They would see God and His angels, Satan and his fallen angels (our enemies), and they would see themselves, their own spirits. They would see the battle positions. What sort of earthly therapy is equipped for such an intense battle? How can the counsel of man avail itself of the Spirit when the counseling stems from the flesh? Prayer, by itself, is not even the answer. The answer is much deeper than all of these things—it lies within the spiritual realm. The key to victory in Jesus is to gain knowledge of God's realm, the spiritual realm where He abides.

The flesh of the natural man (the physical body which is addicted) cannot receive the things of the Spirit of God, because the Spirit of God addresses the man's spirit, not his flesh. That's why we cannot fight spiritual battles with carnal weapons. God was beginning to show me an entirely new approach to winning those battles that would help the people who come to Victory in Jesus meetings, and I was getting a renewed sense of excitement that pulsed from deep within my spirit.

There were two groups that needed God's help; the unsaved in bondage and the Christian in bondage. At first, many were misled into thinking that they were supposed to be addicted in order to attend Victory in Jesus services. But as time passed, they discovered it's for anyone involved in a battle, whether that be for healing, finances, family members, or friends. And I knew they could only receive the message if I preached it by faith into their spirits. I had to believe and practice what I preached in my own life so it would be a living message that I could impart to the people in obedience to the leading and power of the Holy Spirit.

Needless to say, my heart went out to my brothers and sisters in Christ. The need to reach them burned like a fire in my bones. I knew if they could just find out who they were in the spirit they would be able to battle from a victorious position instead of being in slavery to the flesh. I knew God wanted them to be effective, and this meant they would have to be freed!

Before being born again, people don't really experience spiritual problems; their wills are lined up with their flesh, and they are captive to sin. But once a person is born again, and his or her spirit is reconciled to God through the work of Jesus, an entirely new and different scene is set. Suddenly, another voice is heard. This voice opposes the flesh. It's the voice of the spirit-man, the inner man that's now alive to God, and that voice has something important to say. When this happens, a spiritual battle begins, and the flesh goes to war with the spirit-man.

This is what happened to a man named Stan. When they brought Stan to Victory in Jesus, he was burnt out on drugs and he looked like a zombie. They sat him down on the front row and, week after week, he just stared like a statue. The bondage of drug addiction had taken it's toll on him. It looked as if there wasn't much left to this empty shell called Stan.

Some might wonder, "Why preach to a 'mummy'?" I knew I had to preach to him because I knew Stan had a spirit man. His outward appearance didn't amount to much of anything compared to the power of God's Word that I was preaching in faith. I knew the important thing was for Stan to hear a life-changing word. After months and months of being brought back week after week by his concerned family members, the evidence of spiritual transformation began to appear in the physical realm. It was a gradual unfolding.

Stan started to look alive. Then he began to make efforts to repair his broken life. The first accomplishment he achieved was to get his driver's license back. He continued to look more and more alive. We all saw the change and we were so encouraged by it. The Word of God had accomplished its goal. That Word, which is joined to God's Spirit, went into Stan's spirit-man and laid a foundation that enabled him to develop into a productive human being.

This helps us to see that what we sense in the physical realm and believe is real is only a representation; it is only a display of what's taking place in the spiritual realm which we cannot see. This being so, change can only take place by building up the spirit-man, feeding it with the only healthy diet available—the truth of God's Word.

When we fight spiritual problems with spiritual weapons, we can expect the drunkard to stop drinking and we can expect the homosexual or the prostitute, or even the depressed person, to stop practicing sin. When they don't want to do what the enemy tricked them into doing any more, they have found victory.

But what about the captive born-again Christians? Where does he or she fit in? They know something of the warfare, and they are battle-weary. The Lord directed me to teach them how their enemy operates on the battlefield of their minds. They need to learn how to distinguish the voice of the enemy from the voice of God and how to take their thoughts captive to Christ. As they find out who they are in the spirit, victory follows because they have learned to put their spirit in the driver's seat of their flesh and line it up with God's threefold order, that is spirit, soul, and body.

Stan was changed by the power of God's Spirit that was released through the Word of God. In a similar way, we were blessed to see a young woman named Karen find victory in Jesus.

Karen had been born again, but she still faced a fierce battle. She had experienced a dreadful past and the enemy had a lot of material to work with against her. When we met her at Victory in Jesus, she was still in the middle of a battle with drugs.

Realizing she needed some sort of help, she had attended several secular programs. She was trying to get free from the drugs that held her in bondage. She went through rehab programs twice, and each time the insurance company paid $30,000, but Karen remained a drug addict. The battle would be an intense one, but she wanted to fight all the way to victory. She knew that God had a plan for her life, too!

Karen was used to a formula approach to recovery; therefore, when she came to Victory in Jesus she wanted some steps to follow. She wanted to work within a pre-set program. She discovered, at Victory in Jesus, however, that we had only one step—Jesus—and our program was the Bible.

She wasn't happy about it. In fact, she was angry when we wouldn't let her "share" her experience. But Karen was diligent. Each week she attended the regular instruction God provided at Victory in Jesus and, in addition, she faithfully attended two regular church services. Karen's flesh (her natural side) started to bow to the overwhelming power of God's nourishment—His Word for her life.

Something quite different than anything she had ever experienced in all her life started happening to her. Changes began to take place within her. God's Word had found its way into her spirit and its power was radiating into every cell of her physical body. Her spirit was now feasting on the most delicious dinners she had ever had in her life and she was changing from the inside out.

The enemy had dealt Karen such severe blows that she didn't even know how to take care of herself physically. Nancy lovingly taught her about womanly things and Karen kept on progressing. The person who had walked into Victory in Jesus as a disheveled soul was turning into the beautiful creation God had sought for His own glory.

She listened to His Word and she stayed around the right people. We kept encouraging her, and eventually her heart melted before the Lord. Karen discovered that change doesn't have anything to do with steps, her efforts, or even time. Change has to do with diligently seeking God and His timeless intervention into our lives, letting Him perform the plan He has for us.

As she continued going forward in the Lord, she experienced emotional and physical changes that she knew did not come of her own efforts. Being changed from the inside out overpowered her natural side as God spilled His love into her spirit. Today, this lovely woman of God ministers the Gospel to those who are in the gutter of life, a place she's familiar with. Who could know better than Karen what God could do for those "down-and-outers"?

Those are the kinds of miracles we began to see God performing regularly at Victory in Jesus. It was turn-around time for anyone who would drink from the well. God is not like us. He doesn't think that our condition is hopeless. What He knows is that no power can withstand Him.

From the very beginning, I knew my responsibility was to preach the Word of God in faith, but the responsibility for making sure the Body of Christ walks in victory is each believer's. The individual is responsible for his or her own spiritual walk. When people experience spiritual freedom it becomes their responsibility to safeguard it and walk in that freedom.

We need Jesus. Nancy needs Him. I need Him. You need Him. And everyone who comes to Victory in Jesus needs Him. He is the God who is always there. He will never leave us nor forsake us.

God was showing us that spiritual battles, though intense, did not have to be as intimidating as they once had been. He showed me that behind every addiction, every idolatry, every problem, a spiritual enemy was in control. My job was to dethrone that principality and to teach the unsaved and the believer alike how to keep that evil power underneath his or her feet. The power of God's Spirit in me and Nancy enabled us to do it.

We were called to bind up the brokenhearted, to give sight to the blind, and to set the captives free. The anointing to do this was within us because the Spirit of God was within us. In order to minister effectively, we knew that we had to " be strong in the Lord, and in the power of His might" (Eph 6:10). We knew we had to dress in God's armor every day, being sure to put on each piece with prayer. We were equipped by God's Spirit for the warfare, and our responsibility was to obey Him. "For we wrestle not against flesh and blood, but against principalities, against powers, against the rulers of the darkness of this world, against spiritual wickedness in high places" (Eph 6:12).

The most exciting years of ministry were yet to come.

4

Taking Authority

But if I cast out devils by the Spirit of God,
then the kingdom of God is come unto you.
(Matt. 12:28)

Know Your Enemy

The greatest weapon the enemy of God has in his arsenal
is fear. Many Christians fear to confront him because spiritual
warfare is often seen as a "hocus pocus" philosophy that
scares the wits out of anybody, and the enemy likes it that
way. This false approach to the warfare is promulgated by
the enemy himself. Sometimes it even leads some believers
to deny the existence of the devil, and Satan is victorious when
this happens.

So much has been written about horrifying experiences
that Christians have gone through as they've battled with the
enemy that it's no wonder that so many believers want nothing
to do with deliverance. Practitioners of powerless, "hyped-
up" spiritual warfare put people into bondage by causing them
to think that theirs is the work of the Lord when it is quite the

opposite. Often, these approaches are actually witchcraft practiced under the guise of Christianity. "Many will say to me in that day, Lord, Lord, have we not prophesied in thy name? And in thy name have cast out devils? . . . then I will profess unto them, I never knew you" (Matt. 7:22-23).

Our Lord was never beaten by any demon! He was never scratched, bitten, or clawed by one either! As you read on, you will discover that spiritual warfare cannot be waged in the flesh. If you attempt to battle from the realm of your flesh you will be certain to fail. On the other hand, if you battle behind the Lord who abides in the supernatural realm, the result is always victory. There is nothing to fear when you fight the enemy in the power and authority of the Lord.

Spiritual warfare led by our Lord Jesus Christ is always effective and safe. Many do not yet realize that when they sing songs of praise to the Lord that they are battling effectively and spiritually. Praise stills the avenger and the Lord inhabits the praises of the people of God. This is an approach to warfare that brings God on the scene.

The Crossroads of Victory and Defeat

The year was 1990. It was the watershed year I referred to in the first chapter, a year of decision, renewal, and commitment. Nancy and I had been involved in the ministry of Victory in Jesus for five years, but as I mentioned previously, we were standing at the crossroads between victory and defeat. I was clearly tempted to take the road that leads to defeat without realizing its ultimate destination. At the time, it seemed to be the easier of the two roads to follow. There had been many joyous times of victory, but there had been crushing defeats as well.

Instead of counting our blessings, we were counting our losses. We had lost three people to AIDS and one to cancer.

A fine young man had committed suicide by hanging himself, and some of those who had once turned away from drugs had gone back to them. John, the young man I referred to in the beginning of this book, was one of them. His life was grabbed from him by AIDS.

I soon realized that I was taking all of this personally. I thought I had failed these people. There was even a part of me (or a demonic force) that was trying to deceive me into thinking that I had caused these people's failures. "All of this wouldn't be happening," I reasoned, "if I was in the place God wanted me to be [in]." The discouragement was leading me into prayerless depression. My personal hurt had turned to anger, and as always happens, undealt with anger turns into depression.

I began to feel quite alone, except for Nancy's encouraging presence, as I examined my alternatives and wondered what was next for me. I was confused. Unbeknownst to me, it was the most crucial hour of decision I had ever faced.

It was then that I heard God's voice once more: *Vinny, instead of seeking answers, seek me. I have the answers. If you will seek me, you will find the truth. Seek me, and your direction will come.*

Of course. How could I have forgotten this so easily? I had to get back on my knees and seek the Teacher of all Truth. He would show me the steps I needed to take. I didn't realize it then, but God was preparing me for one of the greatest discoveries of my life! He was about to drop an anchor of hope and truth that would hold me secure in all the storms of ministry that would lie ahead. It was an anchor that would find its lodging-place beneath the rock of faith in Jesus Christ and His Word.

As I continued to seek the Lord, the fog of confusion and the clouds of gloom began to lift. The Lord showed me the way through the maze of conflicting emotions, fear, doubt, and depression. It was a time of enlightenment—an awakening—a rebirth. He said, *Vinny, I have given you authority over the enemy. Take your rightful authority over him and you will reach your goal.*

One-by-one, and step-by-step, the Master began to show me the principles I needed to understand in order to win the battle. These foundational truths are the principles I have learned to share with all those who come to Victory in Jesus, and they have made all the difference in the world. Those who follow these steps to victory remain victorious, but those who choose not to avail themselves of these truths will remain in darkness. The choice is given to each one of us, and I'm glad the Lord allowed me to experience the circumstances that led me to these liberating truths, so that I could share them with others. Each of these precepts is based on the truth of God's Word.

The Devil Doesn't Play Games!

"If I did not delight in your law I would have perished in my trial, . . . Thy word is a lamp unto my feet, and a light unto my path" (Ps.119:92, 105, TAB). After John's death, Nancy and I immersed ourselves in the Word of God. In the process, our minds were renewed. We saw all of life—especially our ministry—from a new perspective. So much in life is a matter of focus, after all, and as our focus changed, everything in our lives was renewed. We ministered with greater authority and vitality. The people we ministered to, in most cases, took hold of their responsibilities as believers. As God was magnified, the devil's power weakened. God was becoming bigger and bigger to us as we learned to walk in the light of His truth and power.

Nancy and I learned that we were in a serious conflict with the king of darkness, the prince of the power of the air, the ruler of the darkest domains, the power behind all the darkness in men's hearts and surroundings, causing so much suffering on this earth. He is Satan—the adversary, the one who stands in eternal opposition to God, our Father, and the Lord Jesus Christ, His Son. The "accuser of the brethren" is the "father of lies," and in him there is no light at all. He is like a roaring lion that goes about, seeking whom he may devour. He has no shame, but is filled with pride, hate, sadism, violence, anger, and destruction. He seeks to destroy our ministry and all of the people of God. He wants to replace belief with doubt, health with sickness, life with death, light with darkness, peace with strife, love with hate, and certainty with confusion. Though he is a defeated foe because of Jesus' victory at the cross, he continues to wage warfare in our minds and souls, hoping we'll never find out how to crush his head.

Satan seems to believe that he can still win this battle, but he is wrong. He has a vendetta against the Anointed One, Jesus Christ, and he still desires to occupy the royal throne in heaven. He is opposed to the coming of God's Kingdom, and he seeks to prevent this from happening. His goal is to hinder the Kingdom from coming, and this obsession makes him so "crazy" that he does not care who he steps on to achieve his goals. That's why it takes a command from heaven and a spiritual chain from heaven to bind him and push him into the bottomless pit, when the time comes (See Rev. 20:1-3). But for now, he's confined to one spot (he's not omnipresent), ordering his henchmen around. His evil army consists of powers, principalities, and rulers that he uses to see how much devastation he can cause before he will be tied up and taken totally out of the picture.

Therefore, he uses a myriad of evil spirits who serve as his emissaries for every evil work. Included on his hit-list of would-be victims are those who believe in Jesus Christ and those who would believe in Him. The devil likes to scare us into thinking that he has greater power than the Lord, which he does not. That's why it's important to know what he can do and what he cannot do. He loves to remain hidden and greedily cashes in on our spiritual ignorance.

We cannot play games with such a sadistic enemy, because he is real and he does not play games. Every moment of every day he is seriously preoccupied with the destruction of the Kingdom of God. He is jealous, vindictive, mean, resentful, defensive, and relentless. He despises Jesus Christ and every member of His Church. He loves to inflict harm on the children of God, and he uses every means at his disposal to accomplish these goals. That's why the Lord showed me how spiritual rank and file works.

The first thing He showed me is the seriousness of the conflict. There can be no wimps in the Kingdom of God. We have to be "strong in the Lord, and in the power of His might" (Eph. 6:10). We have to be strong in God if we are going to dethrone the strong man who is a ruler in Satan's kingdom. The Lord told me, *Vinny, you're doing a good job, but you're not completing it.*"

At first this confounded me, and I reacted, "But I'm binding and loosing drug-addicted spirits, alcoholic spirits, pornographic spirits, homosexual spirits, and AIDS spirits."

Yes, Vinny, you are, but you are not getting their boss—the strong man.

Who Is the Strong Man?

The Lord led me to Matthew 12 in order to confirm His word to me and to show me what He meant about overpowering the strongman. "And Jesus knew their thoughts, and said unto them, Every kingdom divided against itself is brought to desolation and every city or house divided against itself shall not stand. And if Satan cast out Satan, he is divided against himself, how shall his kingdom stand?" (Matt. 12:25-26).

I began to see these verses in a totally new light. The Spirit of the Lord showed me that if Satan's kingdom is not divided, it must be well-organized. The kingdom of darkness is far better organized than even organized crime is. It is more organized than the U. S. Army. It follows a clearly delineated chain of command. The devil's army is in perfect rank and file, fully organized for every evil work. Orders are given and carried out in that spiritual realm of darkness in a well-organized fashion. As is true with every army, there are soldiers of various ranks in the devil's ranks. They follow a strict chain of command. They obey their superiors. Each subordinate power is given specific jobs to accomplish according to his rank and specialty.

I found myself thinking, as this realization dawned on me, that it would be so good if the Lord's army was as well-organized, unified, focused, disciplined, and obedient as the soldiers in the kingdom of darkness are. As a matter of fact, the devil has so splintered and divided the Body of Christ that the Church of Jesus Christ, once the great army of God, has been seriously weakened, emasculated, and confused. Brother does not recognize brother. Worse yet, they don't recognize Satan's divisive maneuvers. The most difficult battles occur, not outside in the world but in the Church, as his constant underhanded attacks pit Christians against Christians.

My training continued as the Lord led me through succeeding verses of Matthew 12. "And if I by Beelzebub cast out devils, by whom do your children cast them out? Therefore they shall be your judges. But if I cast out devils by the Spirit of God, then the kingdom of God is come upon you. Or else how can one enter into a strong man's house, and spoil his goods, except he first bind the strongman? And then he will spoil his house" (Matt. 12: 28-29).

The unclean spirit is a designated leader in the spirit-world. He is a ruler who has authority to command cadres of demons who are subservient to him. This is the strongman that Jesus refers to, and he is the one we must dethrone, in the name of the greater One, in order to set a person free. His actions reveal his authorized position and power when he attempts to reenter a person's life again and again even after he or she comes to Jesus.

Next, the Lord showed me the definitive strategy that is behind Satan's attempts to defeat a new Christian who has been delivered from sin or bondage. "When the unclean spirit is gone out of a man, he walketh through dry places, seeking rest, and findeth none. Then he saith, I will return to my house from whence I came out; and when he is come, he findeth it empty, swept, and garnished" (Matt 12:43-44).

The evil spirit had his home in a person and feels like the rest of us. He thinks, "There's no place like home." He endeavors to return to his home, and does so as quickly as possible because, like the rest of us, he does not like being a homeless individual.

Therefore, when the unclean spirit is dispossessed from the house, his field assignment in the devil's spiritual army turns into a retrieval mission. His goal is to reoccupy the house that was "robbed" from him so he can rule again. In order to achieve this, he sets out on a reconnaisance trip to investigate the condition of his former dwelling-place. He recalls the security his familiar surroundings gave to him, so when he sets out on this assignment he takes seven others, more wicked than himself, just in case he will have a fight on his hands in his efforts to reoccupy the person. He does this because when he was forced out of the place, he knew he was forced out by One who is stronger than himself.

For many years the evil spirit was used to controlling the heart and mind and body of the person he formerly inhabited, and he deeply resents being evicted because he lost the use of the physical body, the vehicle he controlled, without which he cannot operate in the physical realm. Because he no longer has a temple (house) to lord over and manipulate, he can't work his assignments on this earth.

God continued to open new realms of truth to me. He said, *Vinny, I know you are familiar with the passage about spiritual warfare in Ephesians 6, but many times you've missed an important truth. When my Word speaks about the rulers of darkness, it is referring to the unclean spirit, the strong man.*

This was a new insight to me. When the strongman seeks to reenter his former home (in the heart and soul of the believer) he can only do so because the house which was swept clean when the Lord entered is still empty. The furniture is gone. The lampstand of truth is missing or has been removed. The foundation of faith has not been built on the Rock of God's Word—or it has been weakened. The rooms are filled with darkness. The joy of a happy home has departed. The banquet table of love is missing. The bed of God's rest has been taken away. The pictures of peace have been lifted from the walls. The person's heart has become more like a dark and empty cave than a house. "Come in, come in," the strong man cries, and seven other devils move in to occupy his familiar home and take up residence with him. "...and the last state of that man is worse than the first" (Luke 11:26).

When the unclean spirit is kicked out, he goes to dry and parched places of the earth. He wants to get back to his familiar surroundings, so he enlists the aid of supporting troops in case there is a battle to be waged. These troops are the seven other spirits that are more wicked than he is. When they occupy the dwelling of a person's soul, they truly trash the place, wreaking havoc and destruction in the realm of that person's will, intellect, and emotions, in order to steal, kill, and destroy their relationships, health, finances, and every other area.

This ruler of darkness—this leader with authority over other wicked spirits—is the strongman. The strongman employs a clear-cut strategy in order to recover all that he has lost. Having been disarmed by the Lord at the person's new birth, or having been caught or cast out, he's unable to reoccupy the individual's spirit which is now permanently reconciled to God. The unclean spirit contents himself, however, with what's left—the person's body and soul. Since he is an evil, driven personality, he doesn't give up. He still seeks to rule the individual, so that he can destroy his or her temple (body) and wreak havoc on his or her mind (soul), doing whatever further damage the individual allows him to do on his eternal way out! The strongman is obsessive and compulsive about reaching this goal.

As this new spiritual understanding came to me, after several weeks of study and prayer, I knew I had found my answer! God had shown me the reason why some who had come through our ministry at Victory in Jesus had fallen prey again to the enemy's devices. It was because the strongman is relentless. He does not give up on his goal. He tries and tries again and again. He keeps losing, but he keeps on trying to regain control. He fights for what he believes should belong to him. Even though he was demoted when he got evicted and humiliated by the presence of Christ, he continues to seek to reclaim "his territory". He seeks embodiment. But when he was evicted, he became limited and could only operate within his designated power spot, the body and soul of a person. Even so, just because he comes back doesn't mean he's supposed to get anywhere, he's just doing what comes naturally to him, and we're supposed to do what comes spiritually to us.

When a person is born again, the unclean spirit loses his control over the person's spirit. When the strongman returns, he returns as a demoted, defeated foe in the spiritual realm. If we could only get a clear understanding of the power of Christ within us! The unclean spirit returns in the guise of oppression, executing a spiritual operation over the soul (the will, intellect, and emotions) of that person, but he cannot possess the reborn person's spirit. He comes back with an attack force and opens fire on the person's mind. That's when we need to recognize him and throw him out. "When a strong man armed keepeth his palace, his goods are in peace: But when a stronger than he shall come upon him, and overcome him, he taketh away from him all his armour wherein he trusted, and divideth his spoils"(Luke 11:21-22).

That's why Christians who were once liberated from all sorts of captivity become slaves to their addictions and problems again. They thought the battle was over when the actual war had just begun. The strong man returned in order to overpower them. They had failed to be vigilant in their watch against him, and most of us don't even know who he is.

Many times Christians fail to defend themselves against him through the power of prayer, Bible study, Christian fellowship, and teaching. They will slack off when the battle is just beginning. When they were born again, they were happy, content, and satisfied with their new-found freedom, but they failed to grow in it. They had not heeded the words of the Apostle Paul: "Stand fast therefore in the liberty wherewith Christ hath made us free, and be not entangled again with the yoke of bondage" (Gal.5:1). They become saved spirits living a life of defeat in the physical realm; totally oblivious to the fact that they have been taken captive by the enemy of their soul. They know they're supposed to be victors but they don't know how to live in victory. Many fail to apprehend the serious commitment the enemy has made to destroy their earthly destinies in God.

Therefore, when the strong man returns he finds the house standing vacant. The dwelling has no truth, faith, love, rest, or foundation built upon the Word of God within it. When the former occupant returns therefore, there is no fight. The enemy simply slips in unnoticed and takes control once more. His nefarious ways are so subtle that they almost elude detection until it is too late—unless, of course, we're aware of him, know how he operates, are able to spot him, fight him, and get the victory over him.

If we don't do this, the strongman and his troops will move with powerful force into an area he really has no right of domain over—your life. Once he's allowed to rule again, he has a literal orgy within the mind and soul of his recaptured home. He and his hordes celebrate their reoccupation of a human soul, and they do so in a very sadistic manner, inflicting pain on the person they now reoccupy. It is as if a riot is taking place within the soul and body. The person who once was free now finds himself in a worse condition than he or she was in before. The unclean spirit who was the possessor of that person is now in the role of the oppressor of that person, pulling him down, as low as he can.

Our task is simple with the Lord's help. It is to heed His Word which describes the strong man's mode of operation and to continue to further strip him and to launch a counter-offensive. We are to become so familiar with his attempts to invade our presence that we must be careful to block and prevent every assault. We must learn to recognize his destructive ways and keep him out. The door to our hearts (where Jesus lives by His Spirit) must remain locked and closed. Signs that say, "God's property—no trespassing—violators will be prosecuted" must be placed on the gates of our minds, kept up, and maintained.

We can't outrun the devil; he has to be faced. We must use our spiritual weapons (especially God's Word) to bind and throw an evil spirit out of our lives and out of the lives of others. A war dance in Church is not going to do it, but exercising the spiritual authority the Lord gave us will!

Only sound teaching, based upon the truthful principles of God's Word, contains God's spiritual power. It can guide us into renewing our minds so we can develop the fruits of love, joy, peace, kindness, patience, gentleness, goodness, faith, meekness, and temperance in our lives. The greatest weapon we have to fight off all would-be invaders is our alignment with the principles of the Word of God. This is the only weapon that is saturated with God's spiritual force; the Bible is the sword of the Spirit. We must ingest His Word (learn how to take the weapon in our hand), meditate upon it (get it sharp in our spirits), and begin to wield it (by binding the unclean spirit) and waging war against our enemy, not against our brother. We must walk in the wonderful light it provides. We must learn to battle and win in the spiritual realm. It was through the Word of God that our Lord and Savior was able to defeat the enemy who came to tempt Him, and through the Word of God in us we will prevail as well.

"Wherewithal shall a young man cleanse his way? by taking heed thereto according to thy word" (Ps.119:9). The

Psalmist learned a lesson that applies to every redeemed and rescued believer today—God's Word will keep us, cleanse us, renew our minds, protect us, feed us, inspire us, lead us, and transform us. We must keep it in our hearts, speak it with our mouths, meditate upon it in our minds, and share it with others. It is the Word of Truth, and the truth sets us free. "Thy word have I hid in mine heart, that I might not sin against thee" (Ps.119:11).

The Word of God is the Rock on which we stand. It is the anchor that holds us secure in the storms of life. It is sharper than any two-edged sword, and it is the source of faith in our hearts. We must stay in the Word at all times.

Our defense is found in the power of the Word of God. We must let it bathe us and clothe us before the crises come. It keeps the enemy out. Light has no fellowship with darkness. The darkness literally despises the light because the light totally dissipates the darkness.

How can the strongman tell that the lampstand of God's Word has been removed from your heart? He can tell by your actions that speak much more loudly than all of your words. He can tell by your reactions to a spiritual attack as well. He watches how you handle every situation that comes up.

Paul shows us how we are to take our stand against the enemy. He instructs us to acknowledge who we are in the spirit-realm and commands us to be strong and stand against the enemy's machinations, his secret plans to achieve evil and illegal ends. The apostle Paul tells us to battle and win, and he tells us how, "Finally brethren, be strong in the Lord, and in the power of His might. Put on the whole armor of God, that ye may be able to stand against the wiles of the devil . . . that ye may be able to withstand in the evil day, and having done all, to stand. Stand therefore, having your loins girt with truth, and having on the breastplate of righteousness; And your feet shod with the preparation of the gospel of peace; Above all, taking the shield of faith, wherewith ye shall be able to quench all the fiery darts of the wicked. And take the helmet of salvation, and the sword of the Spirit, which is the word of God; Praying always with all prayer and supplication in the Spirit, and watching thereunto with all perseverance and supplication for all saints" (Eph. 6:10-18).

The weapon is the Word of God. The shield is faith. The good news is about peace between man and God. The breastplate is our righteous acquittal from the penalty of sin, and the helmet of salvation protects our minds. All of the armor leads us to prayer. We must put on each piece with prayer. We must pray for ourselves and for our brothers and sisters in Christ. We must walk like this, dressed in prayer. And while we're dressed in this uniform we must keep watching and do all of this with all perseverance, so that when the enemy comes we'll wear him out and defeat him sublimely with heavenly power.

More Than One

As God continued to reveal these truths to me, I took a step of faith. Instead of staying at the crossroads of confusion, I made a choice. I would go on. I would continue the ministry of Victory in Jesus. I would obey the Lord.

God was opening our eyes with wonderful light from His Word. Nancy and I were growing together as we recommited our lives to the ministry of Victory in Jesus. It seemed as if we had entered the graduate school of the Spirit of God, and our classload, tests, and expectations intensified beyond all our expectations. It was a time of rapidly accelerated growth that continues to the present day, because it flows in the stream of God's living water—a wellspring of life that produces water that is as clear as crystal from His throne. This water produces fruit. It is the living water of the Word of God, and it was refreshing to be washed clean in its mighty flow.

Everyone, including James and John, the sons of thunder, were amazed by the authority that Jesus displayed as He preached and ministered. He carried out the duties and responsibilities of His rank, and He enjoyed the privileges of His station—His command post. He was a faithful and loyal leader. It was by this authority that He cast out devils. "And they were astonished at his doctrine: for he taught them as one that had authority, and not as the scribes" (Mark 1:22).

This description of Jesus precedes Mark's report about the man with an unclean spirit. It is important to understand that prior to the beginning of His earthly ministry, Jesus had spent more than two decades studying the Word of God and preparing himself to accomplish His earthly destiny.

Jesus walked and talked the Scriptures. He quoted the prophets. He knew the Word of God. He spoke with authority: "Ye do err not knowing the scriptures, nor the power of God" (Matt. 22:29).

Jesus and the Father were communicating as one as He grew in stature and favor with God and men. The Word of His Father had provided the bridge between His humanity and His deity. God's Word was the foundation upon which He built His entire ministry, and He became the Cornerstone that could withstand all the pressure of the entire building that leaned upon it, both then and since then.

"And there was in their synagogue a man with an unclean spirit, and he cried out, Saying, Let us alone, what have we to do with thee, thou Jesus of Nazareth? Art thou come to destroy us? I know thee who thou art, the Holy One of God" (Mark 1:23-24).

The devils recognized who Jesus was in the same way that James and John had done. They recognized the authority in the spirit-realm that was in their presence. They knew Jesus was the Master, the overlord of every situation. Jesus said with authority: "Hold thy peace, and come out of him" (Mark 1:25). In modern-day English this meant, "Shut up! And come out of him." The unclean spirit who inhabited this man begged for Jesus to leave him and his fellow demons alone. He wanted to remain where they were, in their home, where they were comfortable. He was frightened by the spiritual authority of our Lord. He knew he had no power against Him, but he spoke to Him, nonetheless.

Jesus, however, was not about to be dissuaded. He recognized spiritual beings in His presence who were illegally possessing and ruling a human being, and He would not allow them to stay there. He rebuked the evil spirit that had spoken through the vocal cords of the possessed man. He addressed the strong man (the ruling spirit) directly.

He began with a rebuke. This caused an uproar in the spirit-realm. Then, the strong man threw his habitation (the man) to the ground. "And when the unclean spirit had torn him, and cried with a loud voice, he came out of him" (Mark 1:26).

It is vital to notice that Mark had stated (in verse 23) that the man had an unclean spirit (singular). But in verse 24 he reports that the man cried, "Let us alone" (plural).

Jesus went after the strong man, and didn't bother with the rest of the crew the unclean spirit had taken with him into the man. Jesus went for the boss, the prince, the ruler, the ranking official who controlled the demons who lived within this man. Jesus divided, dismantled, and disarmed this strongman's kingdom-of-darkness rule. He did not even address the underlings; He addressed the strong man. He divided and conquered. He executed His superiority, and He left the troops without a leader. When the lesser demons saw their leader surrender (he left as he threw the man to the ground), they had no authority to be there and had to leave too. Jesus conquered the ruling spirit—the one who had been in charge of the man.

Our Lord knew how to operate. He knew that he had to go directly to the boss, and He knew that when He did so, all of the strong man's hideous soldiers would be abandoned and they would have to follow the strong man's departure. This is such an important truth, and Jesus shows it to us so clearly in this passage.

All those who witnessed this in the synagogue were amazed. They asked one another, "What thing is this? What new doctrine is this? For with authority commandeth he even the unclean spirits, and they do obey him" (Mark 1:27).

We see a similar example revealed to us by the Master in Mark 5:1-13, where Jesus is seen dealing with the man of Gadara. "And when he was come out of the ship, immediately there met him out of the tombs a man with an unclean spirit, who had his dwelling among the tombs; and no man could bind him; no, not with chains: Because that he had been bound with fetters and chains, and the chains had been plucked asunder by him, and the fetters broken in pieces; neither could any man tame him. And always, night and day, he was in the mountains, and in the tombs, crying, and cutting himself with stones. But when he saw Jesus afar off, he ran and worshipped him And cried with a loud voice, and said, What have I to do with thee, Jesus, thou Son of the most high God? I adjure thee by God, that thou torment me not" (Mark 5:2-7).

This naked man was demon-possessed. He was a raving lunatic who engaged in self-destructive behaviors of all sorts. He lived in a cemetery. He was so filled with tormenting spirits that he reflected their violence by turning it toward himself and others. No man could restrain him, even with fetters and chains of iron, because his supernatural strength emanated from the spiritual realm and he was, therefore, able to break the links of metal. When he saw Jesus, however, his spirit-man recognized who He was. Nevertheless, he spoke the words that the demons who inhabited the man in the synagogue had spoken. The demons within him were afraid of Jesus. Demons always tremble when Jesus comes, because they know all too well how efficient He is at spiritual warfare. This is why this Gadarene demoniac cried, "Torment me not" (Mark 5:7).

The demon-possessed man was under the authority of an unclean spirit that manifested himself in the natural realm—in the man's outward appearance and behavior. Therefore, it was easy to recognize that he was possessed, unlike the religious man who showed no outward signs of his inward inhabitants. He was able to break natural laws because he was ruled and empowered by an unclean spirit that was subject to spiritual laws, not natural laws. In the spiritual realm, time and all earthly measurements do not exist, and because this is true, supernatural strength can be demonstrated by those who are spiritually empowered. This is true of spiritual power from the dark side as well as the divine side. This possessed man had such supernatural strength that he could break iron in the same way that we can tear a piece of paper.

When the man spoke, addressing Jesus, it was the voice of the strongman speaking through the man's vocal cords. Jesus asked, "What is thy name?"

"My name is Legion: for we are many," the unclean spirit replied.

Jesus was teaching us how to size up the situation, how to discern it spiritually. Jesus was endeavoring to ascertain the command strength of the spiritual entity He was addressing. He was not being polite by asking for the spirit's name. He did not care if the spirit's name was Steve or Alan or Tom, He knew his name was unclean. Jesus wanted him to identify himself—to state his station, his rank, his serial number, as He exposed God's enemy. Following orders, the unclean spirit did not respond with his personal appellation, rather, he told Jesus what his rank and position were. He was in charge of a legion of demons who inhabited this tormented man.

A Roman legion consisted of thousands of human soldiers—from 3,000 to 6,000 foot soldiers, with additional men in the cavalry. No wonder this man could break chains of iron—he was the home of thousands of spiritual soldiers, but Jesus was addressing the one in charge, the ruler, the strong man. The One who would later say, "I have been given all authority and power in heaven and in earth," took charge of the situation. He commanded, "Come out of the man, thou unclean spirit" (Mark 5:8). Notice that even though there were thousands of demons within this man, Jesus evicted the strong man, and all the other demons had to flee with him.

They cried, "Send us into the swine, that we may enter them" (Mark 5:12). They did not want to remain homeless.

Jesus granted their request, and thousands of pigs were crazed as thousands of demons entered their bodies. This caused the swine to run into the sea and drown.

Before this understanding came to me, I had seen legions of demons at work in people's lives, but I did not truly know over whom I should take authority. I remember one man I worked with in 1990. He had committed his life to Jesus Christ after the Lord had freed him from bondage to drugs. But the man's house was unstable, it was not built on the solid Rock of God's Word, so when the floods came he was not able to stand. He had been swept clean by Jesus, but he had failed to maintain the home within his spirit. He failed to make sure it was filled with the things of God. The unclean spirit that had formerly inhabited this man then ordered the low-powered spirits to go back with him to the man. The strongman returned with his companions and knocked on the door. He found the door was slightly ajar, pushed it open, and he and his cohorts moved in to reoccupy and destroy— and that's exactly what they did. I don't know how many new residents came there to dwell, but I saw the after-effects in this man's life. Their partying and wanton destruction led this man into the very pit of hell. He went downhill fast. It didn't take him long to hit bottom. I know because I buried him!

When you receive Jesus Christ as your personal Savior and Lord, you are set free from sin and/or whatever bondage or weakness that has been tripping you up time and time again. It's so critical that you find a church that teaches the Bible, the Word of God. The unclean spirit that once controlled your life will seek reentry, because that's his job, but vital Christian teaching, fellowship, and prayer will help you to keep him away. Your highest priority must be to get your mind renewed, because you have been translated out of the kingdom of darkness and into the Kingdom of God's marvelous light.

God has given you new life and privileges and responsibilities to enjoy and fulfill. As you follow His precepts, the strongman will be defeated each and every time he seeks to control you. "Submit yourselves therefore to God. Resist the devil, and he will flee from you. Draw nigh to God, and He will draw nigh to you" (James 4:7-8). This is the only way to win. God expects you to walk in victory. He wants you to walk in the light that is provided by His Word.

The Word of God will empower you with spiritual authority to defeat all attacks of the enemy. The Word of God is the sword that you will use in dethroning the strongman. The Word of God will give you the spiritual authority that comes from absolute faith—a faith that is more real than anything our minds can imagine.

When you were saved and delivered, Jesus did the spiritual work of binding the strong man as He entered into your heart and your life. He bound the strongman who had previously ruined your life. He kicked out the strongman and the others had to follow him out. When he attempts to come back, however, you must be ready to face him with the Word of God in your spirit-man.

In any time of war, a losing side seeks back-up troops for support. An army needs new and fresh recruits who are not battle-weary. Additional weapons and strategies are required. If you can see this in the light of what it really is, you'll rejoice because it signifies that your enemy is already defeated and wounded; otherwise, he wouldn't be out of the house and he wouldn't need any help to get back in. This is the approach of the strongman. Weakened, he must get support to even approach you again. He feels weak, and he is weak, because he's just been defeated. The general had to surrender. That's why he seeks to order around those who are more evil than himself on the return trip, more evil but still under his authority, in the hope that he won't be recognized for what he really is, a roaring lion with no teeth!

All too often, Christians surrender to the strongman instead of fighting him. A former alcoholic who lets the strongman back into his life may become violent and even commit murder. He may become gravely ill. He could experience a divorce. He may become abusive to others and himself. He may lose his job. He may be involved in a traffic accident, killing others.

In the early eighties, a drunk driver smashed into a school bus that was carrying children and young people from an Assembly of God church in Radcliff, Kentucky. Many of the children were killed. I believe that a strongman in the drunken driver's life had brought wicked forces with him that enabled him to control and empower the driver's body, causing major damage to these precious children who loved Jesus.

Unclean spirits rule spirits of infirmity, spirits of perversion, spirits of excess that always cry for more of some pleasure or addiction. These in turn, wreak havoc in the person's soul, and that person manifests the fruit of the spirit that rules him. If the strongman is allowed to reign, that unclean spirit will oppress the individual until he can manifest in the natural. He will do all that he can to get that person involved once again in the works of the flesh. When adultery, fornication, uncleanness, lasciviousness, idolatry, witchcraft, hatred, variance, emulations, wrath, strife, seditions, heresies, envyings, murders, drunkenness, revelings, and such like are a part of your life, the unclean spirit is achieving his earthly goal of destruction.

In order to avoid all of this, let's make sure our house is firmly standing on the Word of God. We spend a lot of time remodeling and fixing up the apartments and homes we live in. More importantly, we need to do a refurbishing job on the home where the unclean spirit used to live. That house lasts forever—either in heaven or in hell. If we keep our inner dwelling well-maintained and lighted by the Word, when the strongman returns, he'll find a renewed inner man who possesses profound spiritual authority and power in Christ. He won't want to reenter such unfamiliar quarters, because the power of the Spirit of God will send him fleeing. Don't let him ever find an empty house that he can reoccupy.

When it seems that all the forces of hell have gathered around you and Satan violently comes against your life like a flood, remember these words: "When the enemy shall come in like a flood, the Spirit of the Lord will lift up a standard against him and put him to flight"(Isa. 59:19). "Who shall separate us from the love of Christ? Shall tribulation, or distress, or persecution, or famine or nakedness, or peril or sword? . . . Nay in all these things we are more than conquerors through Him that loved us. For I am persuaded that neither death, nor life, nor angels, nor principalities, nor powers, nor things present, nor things to come, nor height, nor depth, nor any other creature, shall be able to separate us from the love of God, which is in Christ Jesus our Lord" (Rom 8:35-39).

Take your authority as a child of God and stand against the wicked one, who will try to deceive you in any way possible. Keep your eyes on Jesus, laying aside every weight and the sin that may so easily beset you, and run the race with the patience that comes from knowing that God has everything in control.

These are some of the first principles that Nancy and I learned during the hour of crisis we faced, and they will work for you as well. We knew from then on that we had to evict the strong man, the unclean spirit, out of each person's life. We also realized that we had to keep our hearts well-furnished with the Word of God. We knew we had to act in faith and walk in love. The next chapter reveals the methods we learned to employ in dethroning the strongman.

5

Dethroning the Strongman

For the weapons of our warfare are not carnal,
but mighty through God to the pulling down
of strongholds; Casting down imaginations,
and every high thing that exalteth itself
against the knowledge of God, and bringing
into captivity every thought to the
obedience of Christ.

(2 Cor. 10:4-5)

Pulling Down Strongholds

The priorities of modern-day society are so out of kilter that people don't even realize that their priorities are listed in the reverse order of God's order and that their values are backwards. Human beings are made in the image of God. Therefore, we are tripartite creatures—spirit, soul and body. God is a Spirit, and His Spirit wants to live within our spirits. God wants to give us guidance for life here on this earth and to preserve us for life in the spirit realm later. God wants us to live with Him through all eternity.

So little emphasis is placed on the spiritual side of life in our present day. Instead of mankind looking at life from a spiritual perspective first, it seems that many people give priority to the needs of the body first. Modern man puts the needs of the body (food, clothing, pleasure, sexuality, exercise) above the needs of the soul (emotional and psychological health, the need to love and be loved) and gives no account to the spirit which yearns for its Maker at every turn. The spirit is the designated leader of the tripartite being. Unfortunately, there is so little teaching on God's unseen realm that it's no wonder why most people give the lowest priority to the needs of the human spirit, which needs the Word of God, faith, prayer, worship, unity with God and the Church.

Some are attempting to meet the needs of the spirit through New Age religions, Native American rituals, Eastern philosophies, romanticism, and the like, but far too often they tap into the wrong authority residing in that realm, without realizing that principalities, powers, and rulers of darkness, that is, all of Satan's kingdom, are spirits as well. The end result of it is that susceptible human beings are taken captive while they are searching for God, because they are unable to discern, to make distinctions in the spiritual realm. When the enemy transforms himself into an angel of light, they can't discern him, so their lack of knowledge about God and the realm in which He abides brings them to their destruction, as it was designed to do. As a result, the true needs of the spirit of man are woefully neglected to the detriment of psychological health, mental health, physical heath, and the well-being of society. Without the God-directed leading of the spirit, man flounders in the physical realm, wondering what life's about, who he is, what his purpose is, etc.

Jesus said, "But seek ye first the kingdom of God, and His righteousness, and all these things will be added unto you" (Matt. 6:33). Therein lies the purpose of man. That is God's direction for us, but most people do just the opposite. They seek material things in an effort to fill the dark void within their spirits, and as a result they become more spiritually ill. God's way is always *spirit first*.

The ancient Greek word for body is *soma*, from which we get our words somatic, psychosomatic, etc. The Greek word for soul is *psyche*, from which we get psyche, psycho, psychology, psychiatry, etc. The psyche is the realm of our emotions, intellect, and will. The Greek word for spirit is *pneuma*, from which we get our words pneumonia, pneumatic, etc.—all of which have to do with breath, air, or wind.

The Scriptures teach us that the Spirit of God is like a wind—a mighty, rushing wind. Jesus compares life in the Spirit to the wind. The Spirit of God is the breath of life in every believer. His indwelling Spirit fills us, energizes us, inspires us, and teaches us. "But if the Spirit of him that raised up Jesus from the dead dwell in you, he that raised up Christ from the dead shall also quicken your mortal bodies by his Spirit that dwelleth in you" (Rom. 8:11). Notice the relationship between spirit, soul, and body in this verse. If the Holy Spirit lives within us, our bodies will be healthier and we will be energized!

Everything in life occurs first in the spiritual realm. Our reconciliation to God, our walk with the Lord, our health, and even our ability to repent emanates in a realm that we cannot see with our eyes. We can, however, see into this realm with the eyes of our spirit. This is what the word *insight* literally means—inner vision. It is the Spirit of God that brings enlightenment to us. He opens our eyes to the truth. This is why the true believer can say, "Believing is seeing," while the world says, "Seeing is believing."

It's all a matter of perspective—it all depends on our focus. Jesus said, "The wind bloweth where it listeth, and thou hearest the sound thereof, but canst tell whence it cometh, and wither it goeth; so is every one that is born of the Spirit" (John 3:8). The context is His message to Nicodemus about the need to be born again. The natural mind cannot comprehend such a phenomenon. Nonetheless, the Spirit of God comes and fills the human spirit like a mighty wind that causes the sails of a ship to breathe with new life, propelling the vessel through the waves with a dynamism previously unknown.

We can't see the wind, but we can hear it. We can't tell where it comes from, but we can experience it. We don't know where it is going, but we can see the evidence of its existence everywhere in the form of falling leaves, spinning windmills, balloons lifting to the sun, trees swaying gently, birds soaring in the clouds, clothing swaying on a line, and kites rising above the beach. The wind is there. It can be felt, experienced, and heard, but it cannot be seen. The same is true with the wind of God, the breath of life, the Spirit of God. He is always there.

Everything happens in the spiritual realm first—even those unwarranted and unexpected attacks of the enemy. Jesus warned us that the enemy would come; He did not say *if* he comes; He said *when* he comes. That's why there are some mornings when you wake up and you feel oppressed or depressed and you begin to wonder if life is worth the struggle. There are times when you, like Nancy and I did during the watershed year of our ministry, feel as if you'd rather switch than fight because you are so weary of the journey and all the battles it entails. It is this spiritual warfare that takes place in the heavenlies that causes some who love Jesus to fall back into a wordly style of life.

There are times when you feel that you can't forgive yourself another time even though Jesus has already done so. I've known Christian men who had felt they had gained the victory over pornography, who in one moment succumbed to the attack of the unclean spirit when he returned to reoccupy their house. The strongman flashed pictures into their minds that these men believed belonged to them. Then, instead of battling with an enemy they could not see, they walked boldly back into an adult bookstore, all the while rationalizing their inconsistent behavior with thoughts like, "Well, God created the human body to be beautiful, so why shouldn't I look at nude people? He created sexuality, so what's wrong with watching people in the act of copulation?" Such a man doesn't recognize the working of an unclean spirit in that case, and the same would be true whenever a believer with a weakness in any given area finds himself/herself falling back into situations from which they had once been delivered.

If this person doesn't increase their knowledge about the spiritual world, a gradual desensitization process goes into motion, and little-by-little, the person loses ground and finds himself falling into the pit of darkness the enemy has reserved for him. It is a dark and fearful place to be. There is no light there, no hope, no motivation to change. The unclean spirit (the strongman) now believes he has succeeded in regaining the territory he once lost, and he begins to establish campaign headquarters in the mind of the unsuspecting victim of his advances. Because he is so familiar with the person he is after, he knows exactly what buttons to push in order to regain entrance. He'll do everything within his power (which is limited, especially by you) to convince you that your justifications and rationalizations are good thoughts. He wants to make you think that the thoughts are yours, that they are reasonable, and that they are good even though the Word of God says otherwise.

Eventually his thoughts will become your thoughts, and you will think the thoughts are yours. His goal is to gain control of your mind. The result is always confusion and depression and guilt, because your mind is being changed by the enemy instead of being renewed by the Word of God. This is serious business.

Single Eye, Single Mind

James writes, "A double-minded man is unstable in all his ways" (James 1:8). This conclusion is drawn by the apostle as he is examining the importance of faith in our lives. Such strong faith is imparted from a single source alone—the Word of God, the holy Scriptures. Paul wrote, "So then faith cometh by hearing, and hearing by the word of God" (Rom. 10:17). It was God's Word that rescued me and Nancy from our time of doubt, confusion, and misguided intentions. When we began to immerse ourselves in the Bible, our vision cleared. We became single-minded in our purpose. Our ways and God's ways, as well as our thoughts and God's thoughts, began to merge. The confusion departed. The fog lifted. The depression and gloom vanished.

God wants you and me to win. This is His purpose for our lives. If you are taught in the faith, it will become action in your life. The Word of God is the only way. His Word gives us faith, hope, and love. His Word enables us to rise above the circumstances of life. The Bible, like an airplane rising above the clouds, lifts us into the realm of sunshine, clarity, fresh air, and warmth. When we are seated with Christ Jesus, our Lord, in the heavenly places, we see everything from a new perspective.

There is no other way. Once you are equipped with God's words, as they are revealed in the Bible, they will take root in your spirit and they will rise up within you when the enemy comes. His words and His Word will militantly conquer. They will send the strongman fleeing. They will be victory in your life. They will impart life. God's Word will prevail in every situation, relationship, and requirement of your life! God's Word cannot fail. It worked for Jesus in the wilderness, for Paul and Silas in prison, for the martyrs of the early church, for Stephen as he faced his executioners, and for believers in every imaginable situation throughout history. His Word will work for you. Live it. Pray it. Appropriate its promises. His words are life and they are victory.

God's Word will equip you to be successful in every onslaught of evil that comes against you. When your enemy returns from dry places, he'll find something new in the place of his former habitation. He won't even recognize his old habitat because he will find a new creature who is controlled by the Holy Spirit in your inner man, and he will see that your mind has been renewed. In fact, your mind will resemble the mind of Christ which is formed in us by the Word of God. Your new mind will fight for all its worth and it will refuse to submit to the devil's devices. Your new mind will recognize his attempts to bring you down. It will refuse to surrender the control of your life.

The renewed mind measures all reality against the principles and the precepts of God's Word. Hence, it is never confused. It maintains a single perspective in single-minded purposefulness. If a given idea or behavior is not permitted by the Word of God, the renewed mind always avoids it. It analyzes every suggestion in the light of God's truth and love. It will counter every attack of the enemy and win because it is rooted and grounded in the Word of God.

The One who is within you is stronger than the one who is in the world. Therefore, when the attack comes, the stronger One in you will surface and your spirit-man will give the orders instead of taking them. That is what we mean by the title of our book and our ministry—there is Victory in Jesus.

The Authority of Jesus

Whenever he was confronted by the enemy, Jesus took action. He always got rid of the unclean spirits that attempted to come against Him. He didn't try to engage in conversation with them in some sort of debate that would attempt to convince them of the truth. He didn't simply pray about them, asking God to make them leave if it was His will. Basically, our Lord and Savior simply took command and ordered the evil spirits to leave!

Essentially, this is the only way to win against such nefarious foes. It is confrontation in the authority of Jesus that enables the believer to win. Such authoritative confrontation is the only way to turn the key in the lock. It is the only means at our disposal to solve the puzzle. The authority of Jesus enables us to untangle the knot, to break the fetters that bind, to set the prisoner free. The anointing of His Spirit is there, as it was with Jesus, to ensure that we will indeed, ". . . preach the gospel to the poor . . . heal the brokenhearted . . . preach deliverance to the captives, and recovering of sight to the blind, to set at liberty them that are bruised, To preach the acceptable year of the Lord" (Luke 4:18-19).

Filled with the Spirit of God and renewed by the Word of God, you will learn how to confront, disarm, expose, debilitate, disable and get rid of every evil spirit in the same way Jesus did. You will discover how to take your rightful authority over them and throw them out! It is the Lord's authority operating within you as a child of God that will enable you to accomplish such feats.

Once you belong to Jesus no unclean spirit has any authority over you. Unclean spirits have no right to manipulate you to influence you. If the strongman comes back in, it's because you let him do so. This happens only when you fail to recognize who you are in the Spirit, and you don't know your name, rank, and serial number in the army of the Lord. In such a case, you fail to perceive your position in Christ. When you know who you are in God, you automatically outrank every ruler of darkness, including Satan himself. It's only when we relinquish control that he is able to steal from us what he once thought was his forever, but the fact is, it never belonged to him in the first place!

All Power in Heaven and in Earth

"Behold, I stand at the door, and knock: If any man hear my voice, and open the door, I will come in to him, and will sup with him, and he with me" (Rev. 3:20). What a wonderful invitation this is, and our gracious Lord extends it to every person on earth. It is important to realize, however, that the One who seeks entrance into our lives, hearts, and spirits is more than "gentle Jesus, meek and mild," a man tenderly caressing a tiny lamb and picking flowers in a beautiful garden. The Jesus who knocks at the door of the human heart is the One who proclaimed, "All power is given unto me in heaven and in earth" (Matt. 28:18). This is not some weak-willed, effeminate, namby-pamby do-gooder. This is Jesus Christ, the Son of God, the One who made all things and in Whom all things consist. This is Emmanuel—God with us. He is the Word made flesh that dwells among us and within us! His name is above every name. At His name demons have to flee, and one day every knee will bow in recognition of His name.

When you opened the door of your heart and allowed Jesus to enter your life, all power in heaven and in earth walked through the door! This is an unyielding power. It does not recognize any higher authority and refuses to bow to any adversary. All power in heaven and in earth dwells within you, because the Spirit of Jesus Christ, our Lord and Savior, lives within your spirit. Now doesn't that change the way you look at the enemy?

"Ye are of God, little children, and have overcome them: because greater is he that is in you, than he that is in the world" (1 John 4:4).

You are "more than a conqueror" through Jesus Christ. You are in Him and He is in you. This is the greatest formula for success known to mankind!

When battles arise and storm clouds threaten, remember Jesus. Remember His authority in you and your authority in Him. When He walked this earth Jesus showed us how to handle the enemy. He made it perfectly clear that unclean spirits have absolutely no authority over us, and at every opportunity He got rid of these unwelcome nuisances who desire to wreak havoc in the lives of people everywhere. Jesus used His superior power to cast demons out. He put them in their place and did not give them an inch. When they tried to engage in battle with the Lord, He put them exactly where they belonged—under His feet.

These emissaries of evil have no rights and privileges in the lives of believers or the members of their families. They have no right to keep loved ones enslaved to alcohol, drugs, pornography, immorality, cigarettes, and perversions. When Jesus is there, these evil spirits have only one choice—and that is to go and never come back! Because we are in Christ, we outrank them in the spiritual domain, and all we need to do is to command them to, " Go, in the Name of Jesus!," and they'll be off to dry places and not around you. They will have no other choice but to go, because within the spiritual realm anything that is not of God is required to submit to Him.

Jesus showed us how to accomplish these victories when He was on earth. That is why the Word of God, in the gospels, devotes so much space to His ministry of spiritual warfare. Evil spirits are real, no matter what science or philosophy say. Jesus provided us with insights into His superior authority over the devil and demons, so that we could appropriate His power when we are in battle. Our Lord and Master proved His superiority in every situation, including circumstances within the natural realm, because He always prevailed in the spiritual realm. He wouldn't yield any ground to the enemy. He refused to share any space with him. Whenever the devil and his cohorts reared their ugly heads, Jesus threw them out like a sack of garbage. For us, therefore, the battle is simply a matter of being like Jesus in all things, obeying His Word, and trusting Him.

Rulers of Wickedness

The spiritual warriors of wickedness are arrayed against the Kingdom of God. They are well-organized according to their various ranks and commands. Unclean spirits hold ranks as ruling spirits and they have authority over other evil spirits which they command to do their bidding. The unclean spirit has authority over spirits of infirmity, drug addiction, alcoholism, homosexuality, pornography, etc. These spirits are the soldiers that are under the command of the unclean spirit. They are so devoted to their rulers that they are willing to be sacrificed if need be like the Kamikaze pilots of World War II.

An unclean spirit does not mind sacrificing one of his underlings if it will further the cause of evil. He will sacrifice a lower-ranking spirit to stay hidden in the abode of the person's life. Through this means the unclean spirit tricks people, including his unwitting victim, into thinking that the "house" has been swept clean.

Nancy and I learned to minister to the people who came to Victory in Jesus meetings by casting out the ruling unclean spirit that inhabits the human spirit of the unsaved and that oppresses the human spirit of the saved. Formerly, we had cast out spirits of infirmity, homosexuality, alcoholism, etc., but the ruling spirit remained behind. No wonder so many folks fell back into sin! They were still controlled by a ruling spirit.

If we don't cast out the ruler, he will continue to deceive, to destroy, and to attack. Before I understood this biblical and spiritual principle, I often found myself confused and defeated. This is why we were so frustrated in 1989 and 1990 that we almost left the ministry, because we had failed to apprehend this truth about spiritual warfare.

It grieved me to see Christians who were dying before their time. I would call the spirit of infirmity out of them, without realizing that I left their boss behind. He continued his nefarious work within their souls. I called out spirits of drug addiction, but the people would get hooked again, and I couldn't understand why. The boss was still there. He would wait until his victim was at a weak moment, and then he would exert his authority over other spirits, commanding them to join him as he returned to that person. The condition of these people would turn out to be at least seven times worse than it had been before.

This is a fundamental truth in spiritual warfare. The devil doesn't want you to understand it. The truth is, however, that the unclean spirit has to leave when you command him to leave. He loses his home, and all the spirits under his control have to go too. It's all a matter of authority. The troops scatter when their leader is missing.

In earthly warfare, when the commanding officer surrenders and raises the white flag, all the troops have to stop fighting. They are under authority. They cannot continue to fight without a leader directing him.

The amazing thing is that since this truth was revealed to me and Nancy, we have not lost a single person to AIDS. As a matter of fact, God has blessed us with numerous miraculous recoveries and progressive healings. This is so different from our ministry in earlier years—especially in the watershed year of 1989/1990, when we lost three people to AIDS, one to cancer, and another to suicide. Those painful losses led me to discover the truth, and as Jesus said, "Ye shall know the truth, and the truth will make you free" (John 8:32).

We need to stop wasting our time with low-ranking privates in the army of Satan and focus instead on their generals—the unclean spirits. Since the Lord instructed me to go after the boss, our ministry has experienced radical results—total transformations of lives that were once so troubled and confused.

We maintain our freedom by furnishing our house with God's Word. This is the key to spiritual growth. Once an unclean spirit is evicted, therefore, and he is replaced with the Word of God, he will know that he is no longer welcome in his former abode. In fact, he will not even want to reenter such a godly abode.

Once he's kicked out, he stays out! Bind the strongman and command him to stay out of your life. Fight like Jesus fought; it's the only way to win, the only way to experience complete victory in Jesus. Remember, the ruler of darkness is no match for the child of God, because you have greater authority in Jesus Christ. "Stand fast therefore in the liberty wherewith Christ hath made us free, and be not entangled again with the yoke of bondage" (Gal. 5:1).

The Enemy's Authority Is Determined By You

There are limits to the devil's authority in your life. Actually, he has no authority at all unless you give it to him. Your authority in Christ far supersedes any authority he has. His power and authority is obtained illegally; it is not rightfully his. Your authority, on the other hand, as a child of God and a warrior of the King, is mighty to the tearing down of strongholds. It is mighty through the Holy Ghost whom Jesus sent to be your teacher and comforter. Nonetheless, the enemy's power is real when he usurps it from a believer. He is shooting with real bullets, and his goal is to control you.

You completely stop his actions in your life when you walk in the faith that is imparted to you from the Word of God. Put God's Word into action in your life. His Word is the sword of the Spirit, sharper than any two-edged sword the devil will try to employ in coming against you. The devil has no weapon to use against faith. "Without faith it is impossible to please him [God]: for he that cometh to God must believe that He is, and that He is a rewarder of them that diligently seek Him" (Heb.11:6).

If you don't believe you will be healed, you won't be, but if you trust God's promises, He will reward your faith. The devil has no weapon against a former alcoholic who reaches for his Bible when the devil tempts him to drink. He has no weapon against the person who latches onto the Word of the Lord and puts it into action in his or her life. The Bible declares, "No weapon that is formed against thee shall prosper, and every tongue that shall rise against thee in judgement thou shalt condemn. This is the heritage of the servants of the Lord, and their righteousness is of me, saith the Lord" (Isa. 54:17).

The Steps of a Good Man Are Ordered of the Lord

Step one - Submit to the Lordship of Jesus Christ. He is your King, your Master, and your Lord. Do His bidding. If He says no, stop. If He says yes, proceed. He will always honor your obedience to His will.

Step two - Understand and accept the Word of God by faith. This requires time to study and to pray. Understanding His precepts is life and wisdom. Following His teachings is peace and joy.

Step three - Follow the footsteps of Jesus Christ. His life is our model in all things—in prayer, worship, spiritual warfare, and holy living. "For even hereunto were ye called: because Christ also suffered for us, leaving us an example, that ye should follow his steps" (1 Pet. 2:21).

Jesus took full authority over the enemy, and we should do so as well. If you want to be like Jesus, take authority over every area of your life. Do not permit any unwelcome guests to enter your life in the form of thoughts, desires, wishes, feelings, or behaviors. When this becomes the stance of a child of God, the enemy will be defeated in his every attempt to undermine the person's faith.

When Jesus taught in the synagogue, the people recognized that He possessed uncommon spiritual authority (See Mark 1:21-23). His teaching was completely different from that of the Scribes and Pharisees. The people could see this contrast in His manner, His words, and in His behavior, and it was readily apparent to the demons of hell as well. After he would teach, Jesus would frequently demonstrate the power and authority He possessed by assailing the powers of darkness. His authority was confirmed as the unclean spirits obeyed His orders. The same demonstration of power and authority is apparent to all when a believer speaks the Word of God in faith. The demons have to flee when the Word is spoken in faith. Every spirit in the realm of darkness knows that such a believer is for real.

Let Us Alone!

"And they were astonished at his doctrine: for he taught them as one that had authority, and not as the scribes. And there was in their synagogue a man with an unclean spirit; and they cried out, Saying, Let us alone; what have we to do with thee, thou Jesus of Nazareth? Art thou come to destroy us? I know thee who thou art, Holy One of God. And Jesus rebuked him saying, Hold thy peace, and come out of him. And when the unclean spirit had torn him, and cried with a loud voice, he came out of him" (Mark 1:22-26).

The man in the synagogue had an unclean spirit, but obviously there was more than one spirit that was tormenting him, and it's interesting to note that they acknowledged Our Lord's deity. The plurality of spirits were under the governance of the strongman, one ruling unclean spirit who knew that the power which would destroy him was issuing forth from the Son of Man, Jesus of Nazareth. Jesus, the man, acted as the vessel for the work of God. Jesus displays the operation of the power of God through his human frame and gives us this example so that we will understand how spiritual authority operates on earth.

Jesus confirmed His authority to the unclean spirit, the lesser spirits, the people who were in the synagogue, and us. All the rank and file of hell had to submit to His orders. This is the exciting reality that takes place every time the Word of God goes forth in faith. Every spirit in the spiritual realm is defenseless against the Word of God. When you use the Bible as your weapon, every spirit will know that your faith is for real; it is strong, powerful, and authoritative.

The man in the synagogue cried out, "Let us alone; what have we to do with thee, thou Jesus of Nazareth? Art thou come to destroy us?"(Mark 1:24). The ruling unclean spirit was hiding in the man. He did not speak. He was attending synagogue with the man! Collectively, the spirit underlings spoke through the man. The strongman was not alone.

Jesus did not respond by addressing the group of spirits who inhabited the man, however. He spoke to the ruling spirit—the unclean spirit, the strong man. "And Jesus rebuked him, saying, Hold thy peace, and come out of him"(Mark 1:25). He spoke directly to one spirit, not many. Jesus stopped the lesser spirits from talking, went after their leader, and proceeded to throw out the strongman who had been hiding, not talking.

When Jesus got rid of the boss, the others had to leave. The people who witnessed this exorcism were amazed by the spiritual authority that had been demonstrated in front of them. The devils were concerned about the time of judgment—they did not want to be destroyed. These evil beings do know their future.

In Matthew 10:1, we see that Jesus empowered His disciples to do the same work He did. "And when he had called unto him his twelve disciples, he gave them power against unclean spirits, to cast them out, and to heal all manner of sickness and all manner of disease"(Matt. 10:1). This is what Jesus called them to do, and He backed them up with the power to accomplish these purposes. He has called us to do the same, and He has imparted the strength of His Spirit to enable us to do so.

Why Some People Lose Their Healings

Notice the order of the preceding verse. Jesus gave His disciples power against evil spirits first, then power to heal. This is important. First, we bind and cast out the unclean spirit, then we minister God's healing power. If we attempt to bring healing first, the unclean spirit will continue to hide, waiting for the opportunity to manifest himself at some future time. This is the reason why some people lose their healings.

We see this, also, in Luke 13:11-16, when Jesus handled the situation with the woman who was bowed over for eighteen years; He was moved with compassion. "And when Jesus saw her, he called her to him and said unto her, Woman, thou art loosed from thine infirmity." First, he loosed her from the spiritual attack. "And he laid his hands on her: and immediately she was made straight, and glorified God." Then He took His hands and healed her. This all started because ". . . he was teaching in the synagogue on the Sabbath. And, behold, there was a woman which had a spirit of infirmity eighteen years and was bowed over together and could no wise lift herself up."

Soldiers, as we have just learned, have no authority except that which is given to them. How was it possible, then, for a spirit of infirmity, who is a low-ranking soldier, without any authority, to be able to function without a leader? Where was the unclean ruler spirit in the case of the woman who was bowed over? Right after the woman was healed, the ruler of the synagogue became indignant. He was angry that the healing took place on the Sabbath. Then Jesus unmasked the ruler in the picture when He responded to the leader by saying: "And ought not this woman, being a daughter of Abraham, who Satan hath bound, lo, these eighteen years, be loosed from this bond on the Sabbath day? Satan ruled this one himself! There's always an unclean spirit behind the problem.

The unclean spirit is willing to sacrifice a spirit of infirmity or other lesser spirit in order to keep control of the person. He deceives his victim by letting him/her receive a temporary healing, but the need for complete spiritual healing remains unmet because the unclean spirit still maintains his residence within the person. He surrenders at one skirmish on purpose in order to have a chance to win another battle later.

Jesus always went after the strongman first. He knew He had to get rid of the leader in order for the healing to be complete. He uprooted the unclean spirit and ministered healing to the victim.

The strongman will feed on an individual's lack of application of the Word of God. He doesn't want you to find out about him. He doesn't care if you come against lesser entities because he knows the spiritual progress you will make with such an approach will be only temporary. He also knows the spiritual progress of the person he's trying to control will be hindered if the unclean spirit remains undisturbed and is allowed to control the individual at a close range. He will wait until the time is ripe in your life, and then bring in additional forces that will revel in their destruction of your life.

An absence of the Word of God equals a lack of knowledge of God, and that is a dangerous situation to be in. God wants to transform us into the image of Christ, if only we would give Him the chance. That is His goal. Spiritual progress is the way of the Lord. His intention is to build on His foundation and bring us into an accurate understanding of His Word. That can only happen as we yield to Him and allow Him to discipline us into that which He would have us to be. As we progress, God brings us forward into a better and more-accurate understanding of His ways and principles. But He needs our cooperation in order for Him to accomplish this work. It is for this reason that God will never send you to a higher level until you gain the knowledge presently at hand. Our Lord is seeking to save us not only at the time of our deaths but also at every impasse we face in our earthly lives. We must begin to lean on Him.

"When the unclean spirit is gone out of a man, he walketh through dry places, seeking rest, and findeth none. Then he saith, I will return into mine house from when I came out, and when he is come, he findeth it empty, swept, and garnished. Then goeth he, and taketh with himself seven other spirits more wicked than himself, and they enter in and dwell there: and the last state of that man is worse than the first" (Matt. 12:45).

Carnal Christians (those who live in the flesh) are manipulated by unclean spirits. They don't even realize that they are under the control of a strongman. They continue blindly in their sin and selfishness, thinking all the while that they are good Christians.

When the epileptic boy was brought to Jesus, the unclean spirit threw the child to the ground and he went into convulsions. Jesus rebuked the unclean spirit and the boy was completely restored to health. The unclean spirit did not say a word to the Lord, but Jesus knew about Him through the spiritual gift of discerning of spirits (See 1 Cor. 12:10).

At Victory in Jesus meetings, when an alcoholic spirit or a drug-addicted spirit speaks to me and says, "I'm an alcoholic" or "I'm a drug addict, " I usually respond, "I know that, and you're going to come out of this man/woman, along with your leader." This is a fulfillment of Zechariah's prophesy: "And it shall come to pass in that day, saith the Lord of Hosts, that I will cut off the names of the idols out of the land, and they shall no more be remembered: and also I will cause the prophets and the unclean spirit to pass out of the land" (Zech. 13:2).

This is the destiny to which we have been called. The Lord will cause the unclean spirit to pass out of the land. The names of the idols will be cut off and they will not be remembered. God will strip the unclean ruler spirit of his control in the lives of individuals, families, and throughout the land. That will be a glorious day, and we believe the day of victory has begun. It is only the Body of Christ that can thwart the works of the enemy. The Word of God exposes the unclean spirit for what he is. As believers act upon the Word, and put it into effect in their own lives and their ministry to others, the unclean spirit will be disarmed. Eventually he will no longer have control over our nation, our communities, our families, our institutions, and our personal lives. Believers will bind him and loose him because they have infinitely more power than he has. When we operate with one heart and one mind in one Spirit, under one Lord, the Kingdom of God will advance beyond all expectations!

At Victory in Jesus, we are learning how to regain lost territory in the lives of those we minister to. It is such a joy to see lives reclaimed through the power of Jesus Christ. In the next chapters you will meet some of the people who have found total victory by pulling down strongholds that had long held them captive.

6

Crossing the Bridge

While we look not at the things
which are seen, but at the things
which are not seen: for the things
are seen are temporal; but
the things which are not seen
are eternal.

(2 Cor. 4:18)

Bridging the Gap

God's ways are not our ways, and His thoughts are not our thoughts. The ancient prophet Isaiah pointed this out in Isaiah 55:8-9. People who come to Jesus have walked out of the kingdom of darkness (ruled by Satan) and walked into the Kingdom of God. Their ways of thinking, living, feeling, believing, and behaving undergo a radical adjustment process. Always before they looked at everything from a natural perspective; now the eyes of their spirits have opened, enabling them to see spiritual truths.

Throughout their lives previously they had no conception of the unseen world of the spirit. Now it has become very real to them. They have begun to walk across a bridge that spans the gap between God's ways and our ways, God's thoughts and our thoughts, and the spiritual world and the natural world.

My forebears were from the lovely little country of Italy. In Venice, the city of canals, there is a bridge that is known as the Bridge of Sighs. It is called the Bridge of Sighs because it was the bridge that led from freedom to darkness, just the reverse of the bridge that leads out of darkness into light. Prisoners had to cross the Bridge of Sighs as they were led to the dark and dank dungeons of the city where they would spend the rest of their lives. Frequently they would pause at a little window placed in the middle of the covered bridge and they would sigh deeply, realizing that the world of light and freedom was behind them and a world of total darkness lay ahead.

The spiritual bridge that a new Christian crosses could be called the Bridge of Life, because it leads one out of the dungeons into the Promised Land of God's continual blessing. However, there are some who endeavor to cross this bridge, and, like Lot's wife, look back longingly at the sins of the past. These individuals may sigh as they cross, and even if they make it to the other side, they may wonder if they've made the right decision. Whatever the case, those who cross the Bridge of Life face many adjustments in every area of their lives.

Faith for the Change

Faith is the greatest tool we have at our disposal. When we are born again and our spirit is made alive to God, we receive a measure of faith that helps us to know that God is real, that Jesus died for us and rose again, and that He lives within our hearts. We begin to accept the reality of the unseen world.

"Now faith is the substance of things hoped for, the evidence of things not seen" (Heb 11:1). The individual who accepts Christ as his/her Savior begins to understand that the real person (the new man) who lives within them is an eternal Spirit that cannot be seen. The truth must be accepted by faith, and not by sight. In the Kingdom of God, therefore, believing is seeing, but in the natural world seeing is believing. Everything changes for the person who crosses the bridge.

Things that we see in the natural realm are subject to the things that are unseen in the spiritual realm. That is what spiritual warfare is all about. Whereas an individual may have been addicted to a substance, person, or behavior in the natural realm, held captive for a long time, he or she has found strength to put the addiction behind them—a strength that comes from the spiritual world.

This is possible because a greater force is at work within them. "Ye are of God, little children and have overcome them: because greater is he that is in you, than he that is in the world" (1 John 4:4).

Temporary Setbacks

Many people begin their new life with Christ with great vitality and joy. They feel empowered and consider themselves dead to sin. It is as if they have entered a beautiful garden that is fruitful and fertile, and all they have to do is pick the fruit from the branches of the tree. This is a common experience for those who find Christ.

Unsuspectingly, these new converts may forget that there is an enemy that seeks to devour them. He wants them to partake of the fruit of the Tree of Knowledge of Good and Evil, which will kill their innocence and banish them from the Garden. This happens when the individual's defenses are down, usually due to negative and difficult circumstances that come their way.

Satan wants the former addict to lose hope, and his greatest weapon is discouragement. It seems as if he reasons, "If I can get the person to go back to the natural way of thinking, I will be able to ensnare him/her again." When the individual buys into this temptation, he/she will frequently fall back into the addictive behavior. This is where Christian fellowship takes a vitally important role in the new believer's progress. Christian fellowship, many times, can be the sustaining factor in a new convert's spiritual walk.

Paul wrote, "Brethren, if a man be overtaken in a fault, ye which are spiritual, restore such an one in the spirit of meekness; considering thyself, lest thou also be tempted. Bear ye one another's burdens, and so fulfill the law of Christ"(Gal. 6:1-2). When we see this backsliding process taking place in a believer's life, we who are spiritual (meaning those who have walked closely with the Lord over an extended period of time) do have an important responsibility to fulfill in the lives of our brothers and sisters.

We can help to restore them to fellowship with God and with their fellow-believers. We can show them that their failure is only a temporary setback. We can bear their burdens through prayer, love, counseling, spiritual warfare, speaking the Word of faith, being an example of godliness, and teaching them the truths of the Bible. When we do this, we are fulfilling the law of Christ, which is love.

The goal is to keep them focused on the things of God. We remind them that they can exercise the gift of faith that has been imparted to them by believing the truth instead of a lie. God has promised to keep on changing them as long as they pursue spiritual development by studying the Word of God, praying in faith, and living righteously.

When God created the earth He did so out of the dark void of the universe. He commanded the heavens and the earth into existence by the authority of His Word. He said, "Let there be light," and there was light. He literally spoke the worlds into existence.

The Word of Faith Is Near You

"The word is nigh unto thee, even in thy mouth, and in thy heart: that is, the word of faith, which we preach"(Rom. 10:8). When we speak the word of faith, newness of life is created around us. This allows us to see things from a spiritual perspective, not a natural one. We rise above the temptations, pressures, circumstances, and feelings of life.

Paul went on to explain, "For with the heart man believeth unto righteousness; and with the mouth confession is made unto salvation" (Rom. 10:10). Faith begins in our heart (spirit), and it is released through positive faith. If we are saying negative things (even in the form of messages we give ourselves mentally), we will reap a harvest of negativity. If we speak faith, however, new strength and life flow into our spirits and bodies.

In the act of creation, God showed forth His mighty power in more ways than one. For one thing, creation teaches us that the realm of the spirit does, in fact, exist, and that it has the power to create new situations out of old ones. The chaos was replaced by order. The darkness was replaced by light. The emptiness was replaced by abundance—the fullness of creation. God moved by His Spirit and the universe was brought into being.

Faith changes situations when we trully believe and utilize it. God created the universe—the sun, the planets, the moon, the stars, the seas, the continents, the rivers, the lakes, the mountains, the trees, the animals, and us—by His authoritative command. He made us in His image; therefore, we are creative beings as well as created beings. We can exercise divine authority over this life. As a matter of fact, God clearly states that He gave us this authority: "Be fruitful and multiply, and replenish the earth, and subdue it: and have dominion over the fish of the sea, and over the fowl of the air, and over every living thing that moveth upon earth" (Gen. 1:28). God wants us to take charge of everything around us. He has given us the authority to do so.

Someone you can't see created everything that you can see. He did so out of the substance of the spiritual world. Hebrews 11:1 tells us that faith is the substance of things hoped for, the evidence of things not seen. This speaks of spiritual substance. Faith is based on this firm foundation of spiritual substance that cannot be seen. This kind of faith has great power in a person's life.

A major part of crossing the bridge, therefore, is simply to believe. "But without faith it is impossible to please him; for he that cometh to God must believe that He is, and that He is a rewarder of those who diligently seek Him" (Heb. 11:6). The Bridge of Life, then, is constructed with the building blocks of faith. It is the bridge that takes us from darkness into light, death into life, despair into hope, defeat into victory, discouragement into courage, and confusion into certainty. It leads to an entirely new realm of living—a higher dimension and quality of life on this earth, as well as in the life hereafter.

The Faith of God

The faith of God never doubts. It is certain with regard to God's promises. It is security in its highest form. Jesus speaks about the faith of God in Mark 11:22-24: "And Jesus answering saith unto them, Have faith in God. For verily I say unto you, that whosoever shall say unto this mountain, Be thou removed, and be thou cast into the sea, and shall not doubt in his heart, but shall believe that those things which he saith shall come to pass; he shall have whatsoever he saith. Therefore I say unto you, What things soever ye desire, when ye pray, believe that ye receive them, and ye shall have them."

Over and over again Jesus urges us to believe. This is the key. This is the God-kind of faith. It trusts. It believes. It does not question. It does not doubt. It clings to God in faith.

Have faith in God. (This was Jesus' commandment.) He will do whatever He promises. He will be faithful to His Word. He will bring it to pass. He is the Giver of every good and perfect gift. Draw near to Him. He will meet your needs.

There is no unbelief in the faith of God. When we join our faith with His, we are greatly empowered to deal with any issue of life. It's such a wonderful life, this walk of faith. Nothing in all the world can compare to it. The faith of God is a gift of spiritual power that creates miracles and healings. It is a faith that can literally move mountains because it is rooted and grounded in the Word of God and in His love.

The way to use God's powerful faith is to believe His irresistible words. This special gift of faith enables you to believe God for the impossible. Peter used the faith of God in Acts 3 when he encountered the handicapped man at the gates of the Temple. The man asked for money, but Peter said, 'Silver and gold have I none; but such as I have give I thee: In the name of Jesus Christ of Nazareth rise up and walk"(Acts 3:6). Immediately, the man's feet and bones received strength.

It wasn't about silver and gold: it was about a far greater gift—the miracle-working power of God. This shows us what the faith of God can do. God's faith can change any seemingly impossible situation. It prevails in the face of every obstacle. It is a faith that overcomes adverse situations. It is the faith of God.

Faith Leads Us Into the Presence of God

How can any Christian stand in opposition to the people of God growing in faith? The devil wants to keep us from progressing in the life of faith. Sometimes he will even use Christian leaders to hold us back. Our attitude, however, must continually be one of perseverance. "Wherefore seeing we also are compassed about with so great a cloud of witnesses, let us lay aside every weight, and the sin which doth so easily beset us, and let us run with patience, the race that is set before us, Looking unto Jesus the author and finisher of our faith; who for the joy that was set before Him endured the cross, despising the shame, and is set down at the right hand of the throne of God" (Heb. 12:2).

Faith is God's mighty, active substance, and it is what He uses to bring change on the earth. This is one of the reasons why He prescribes prayer as a means for spiritual growth in our lives. He always responds to believing prayer!

Trees Without Fruit

Jesus said, "I am the true vine, and My Father is the husbandman. Every branch in me that beareth not fruit he taketh away: and every branch that beareth fruit, he purgeth it, that it may bring forth more fruit . . . Abide in Me, and I in you. As the branch cannot bear fruit of itself, except it abide in the vine; no more can ye, except ye abide in Me. I am the vine, ye are the branches. He that abideth in Me, and I in him, the same bringeth forth much fruit: for without me ye can do nothing. If a man abide not in Me, he is cast forth as a branch, and is withered, and men gather them, and cast them into the fire, and they are burned. If ye abide in Me, and my words abide in you, ye shall ask what ye will, and it shall be done unto you. Herein is My Father glorified, that ye bear much fruit, so shall ye be my disciples"(John 15:1-8). Jesus is the vine; we are the branches. He lives in us; we live in Him. His life coursing through our veins produces lasting fruit when we continue to abide in Him. Our fruitfulness glorifies the Father.

Many oppressed and addicted individuals have gone to religious institutions in order to find freedom, but so many have left even more depressed than they were when they went. Many walk away still captive, and some even blame God for their predicaments. Homosexuals, for example, may cry, "This is the way God made me." An alcoholic may attempt to justify his/her condition by saying, "I was born with an alcoholic gene." Drug addicts may try to reason as follows: "This is the way my mother was; therefore, God must want me to be that way, too."

On the surface, the statements may seem to hold some truth because the behaviors and orientations are so deeply ingrained within the person's psyche that they no longer have any idea of when the problem began. The spiritual aspect is seldom taken into consideration. So much in our society today, thanks to Dr. Sigmund Freud, is focused on psychology and psychiatry. These "sciences" attempt to explain every human condition.

If the drive for immediate gratification comes from my *id* (my inner child, the pleasure principle within me), it is beyond my control. There's nothing I can do about it. If it gives me pleasure, what's wrong with it? It's just the way I am. "I gotta be me." These are lies from the pit of hell.

The Bible promises us new life. The Bible says we can renew our minds. When we come to Christ, the old has passed away. Paul wrote: "Therefore if any man be in Christ, he is a new creature: old things have passed away; behold, all things have become new" (2 Cor. 5:17). We don't have to stay in the old ruts. We can change completely through the power of God, if we will learn to walk in His Word and let His faith transform our lives, our thinking, our focus, our relationships, our behaviors, our goals, and everything else.

One man who came to Victory in Jesus had been on drugs for over twenty years. He had watched some of his friends go to jail, others die of overdoses, and a few develop AIDS. He tried several secular, twelve-step programs in order to find freedom, but each attempt was to no avail. He then turned to the church he had attended as a boy. He was scared and he hoped God would help him. He did not want to go to jail, he did not want to die from an overdose, and he did not want to get AIDS.

His heart was filled with hope as he went to his family's church. He was certain that he would find the answers he needed there, but just like it had been in the recovery programs he had attended, he went in as a drug addict and came out as a drug addict. Regrettably, they did not have the resources to help this desperate man.

He considered his condition to be totally helpless, until one Easter when his sister invited him to attend church with her. Her church was different from the one he had known as a child. The people there preached the Word, worshiped God freely and audibly, and they loved one another. For the first time in his life, this thirty-something-year-old drug addict heard the Word of God preached with faith and authority. His spirit stood at attention. He listened and soaked in the hope of the Gospel. When the invitation to receive Christ was extended to the congregation that Easter Sunday morning, this man went forward. His heart was pounding, and he felt like skipping to the altar. He accepted Christ as his Savior and Lord, and then he was directed to the prayer room where he received the Baptism in the Holy Spirit.

The leader who prayed for him encouraged him to attend Victory in Jesus meetings, and this newborn babe came to every meeting. He was a sponge that soaked up the Water of Life. He was completely transformed by the power of God. His faith grew and grew. In our meetings he met a beautiful young Christian lady who became his helpmate in Christian service. He found a steady job, grew in the grace and knowledge of the Lord, and now he and his wife are living for Jesus as they parent the sweet baby girl that God gave them. This is the power of God at work in the twentieth century.

Some will try to teach that gifts and miracles of the first-century church are passed. They say that the Book of Acts was for an earlier dispensation. I know that they are wrong. At Victory in Jesus we are seeing dramatic healings, radical conversions, total transformations, full deliverance, and complete victory occurring in people's lives every week. Many of these folks were considered to be the dregs of society before they came to us; now they are lights in the darkness. They are fruitful trees in the Garden of God.

Trees without fruit are useless, but fruitful trees reap a luscious, nutritious, bountiful, and prosperous harvest. God wants us to be fruit-bearing Christians every day of our lives. In the Parable of the Fig Tree, Jesus reveals the importance of this truth; "And when he saw a fig tree in the way, he came to it, and found nothing thereon, but leaves only, and said unto it, Let no fruit grow on thee henceforward forever. And presently the fig tree withered away"(Matt. 21:18-19). Jesus was hungry, and He desired fruit from the tree. The fig tree had many leaves which are designed to protect the fruit from the sun and other elements, but when He lifted its leaves, He could find no fruit! The tree looked good from a distance, but upon closer examination, it was useless. And so it is with many religious institutions. Where is their fruit? What kind of harvest do they reap?

The drug addict I referred to above was looking for fruit. When he thought about returning to God, he reasoned that the best place to go to find Him would be the church of his youth. It looked nice, with its stained-glass windows, marble altars, beautiful statues, magnificent painting, and nicely carpeted aisles. The music was refined and artistic. The vestments of the clergy gave them a very religious appearance, but there was no fruit there. The church could not help him. The pastor could not help him. The people could not help him. The music could not help him. There was no fruit on the vine.

The absence of these vital qualities is rooted in the absence of faith. Some institutions have an appearance of godliness, but they deny God's power. Such churches and agencies cannot really help anyone. Their fruit will not remain. This is why we see so many people coming to us from mainline denominations with elaborate Gothic cathedrals which are powerless to help those who really need divine intervention. All too often, faith is inoperative in such a setting. Sometimes it is an unknown entity.

James writes, "Faith without works is dead"(James 2:20). By the same token, works without faith are dead as well. Works that stem from faith, however, always produce lasting fruit. It's vitally essential to put faith to work in a addicted person's life. Without it, the person will become like the fig tree Jesus cursed. The tree withered and died. The key to producing long-lasting fruit, as Jesus pointed out, is to abide in Him and to let His words abide in us. Then, we will ask whatever we will and it shall be accomplished. If we fail to abide in Him, though, we are cast forth as a branch, and when this happens we wither and die (See John 15:1-8).

God's Word Produces Life

The Word of God brings forth life. An environment of faith helps people to grow, in the same way that an emerging bud blossoms into a flower in the sunshine of God's love. The flower becomes an attractive fruit that makes people hungry for the things of God. This takes place as a spiritual process in a human being, and we have been priviledged to see this happen many times at our Victory in Jesus meetings.

Once, for example, a go-go dancer from a nearby club came to one of our Tuesday evening meetings. She had a long career in her field, and she had danced in several different night clubs. She learned to love to hear the Word of God preached in faith and authority, and she continued to attend our services. It was then that something quite unexpected happened to her. Every time she would perform at the club, a heavy spirit of gloom and depression would envelope her. She began to hate doing what she once loved to do. As she would dance in front of the leering men, the Word of God would leap up within her and she would feel convicted and ashamed. It would fill her with revulsion every time she would gyrate before the men in her scanty outfit. She was embarrassed by the cheers and catcalls that used to make her feel proud. She wondered if she was going through a nervous breakdown.

What she didn't realize was that the buds of life were turning into blossoms. They wanted to bring forth fruit, and as soon as she understood what was happening, she knew she had to leave her "profession". One night, under the strong conviction of the Holy Spirit, she walked out of the night club and closed the door on that life-style forever. She also closed the door on the alcohol and drugs that had always been so much a part of her life.

She continued to be a faithful member of our Victory in Jesus brigade and led many others to a saving knowledge of Jesus Christ. This beautiful woman became ever more beautiful as she radiated the love of God from her innermost being. Eventually she met and married a man who attended our meeting and had been delivered from drugs and alcohol. Now they serve as youth ministers in another state.

We had simply preached the Word of God in faith with authority. She heard the Gospel, and the seeds we sowed found a place in the soil of her heart. God gave the increase, and now the former stripper is sowing seeds of faith in the hearts and lives of other troubled souls. God is so good to us. This couple is our son and daughter-in-law!

Fruit-Bearers, Not Fruit Inspectors

Our job as believers is to bear the fruit of the Spirit wherever we go. It is not our responsibility to be judgmental, but discerning. Jesus said, "Ye shall know them by their fruits. Do men gather thorns, or figs of thistles? Even so every good tree bringeth forth good fruit, but a corrupt tree brings forth evil fruit. A good tree cannot bring forth evil fruit, neither can a corrupt tree bring forth good fruit. Every tree that bringeth not forth good fruit is hewn down, and cast into the fire. Wherefore by their fruits ye shall know them" (Matt 7:16-20).

When we wonder about the kind of church we ought to be attending, there is really only one question to ask: "What is the fruit of that church?" When I lived in Arizona, a state that produces many citrus fruits, like Florida and California do, I would often pass by lemon orchards on my way to work. I would see men working among the trees, but I could not see the trees' fruit. Had I stopped and asked these men, they probably would have explained that it wasn't time for the trees to produce fruit, but when the harvest time comes, I would be able to see the finest fruit trees ever produced!

It is the same in the spiritual realm. The farmers and laborers in the orchards are employing faith as they continue to work and wait for the harvest. They plant the seeds, nurture the trees, prune them, and God gives the increase. They work every day in the full expectation that the time of fruition will come. They don't only believe it; they *know* it! If they didn't fully accept it, through faith and former experience, they would not work so hard at cultivating the crop.

A few months later, as I would drive by, I could see bright yellow fruit decorating the boughs of the trees. It was so beautiful to watch the natural transformation that took place at the hands of God, who continues His workmanship through His managers—the farmers and the hired hands. It is the same in the Church. Nancy and I plant seeds, we cultivate the crop through the Word, and God gives the harvest. It is so beautiful to behold His redeeming, transforming, and liberating work in the life of a believer. Many of the people who come through Victory in Jesus become trees that are truly laden with fruit.

In Arizona there were lemon trees, orange trees, tangerine trees, and grapefruit trees. Once their fruit emerged from the branches, it was not difficult for me to discern which was which. Without the fruit, however, it was very difficult for me to discern the kind of tree I was looking at. It is the same in the Kingdom of God. When the fruit emerges, we know. If it is bad fruit, we know the tree is not planted properly in the ground of God's Word. If it is good fruit, we know God is blessing it.

Amaziah was a King who did what was right in the sight of the Lord, but his heart was not right before God. His motives were impure. There was guile and deceit where love and faith should have been. Nonetheless, he was able to reflect some of the things of God in his life. It is this way with some ministries today as well.

If we are only a reflection of the truth, then we are not emanating the truth from our innermost spiritual reservoir. Reflected truth does not bring forth good fruit that will last. Real truth does. Only the real thing, Jesus said, will produce good fruit. I can hang fruit on a tree with a string much like one might decorate a Christmas tree, but that fruit will not remain, it will wither and die. It will get rotten. But if the fruit comes forth from a life and ministry that is hidden with Christ in God, its fruit will remain.

Only mature trees produce good, healthy fruit. They need to be groomed, pruned, cultivated, trimmed, fertilized, watered, protected, and nurtured before they can be ready to be fruitful trees. It is the same in the spiritual realm. Fruitfulness happens as believers are washed and nourished by the Word of God. Paul wrote to Timothy, his young son in the faith, "Study to show thyself approved unto God, a workman that needeth not be ashamed, rightly dividing the word of truth" (2 Tim. 2:15).

I've seen impatience devour many a new believer because they failed to get grounded in the Word of God before attempting to launch out in ministry. The way to develop a fruitful ministry is to get grounded in the Word of God, to let it wash you clean as it renews your mind and bridges the gap between your way of looking at things and God's. God's Word will keep you from sin, and sin will keep you from God's Word. If the Word isn't as meaningful to you now as it once was, then something is wrong in your life. God's Word is truth, life, bread, water, and spiritual growth. It is an infallible rule for faith and practice in our lives. It is our guidebook, manual, directory, dictionary, encyclopedia, and atlas.

Jesus said we must abide in Him and let His words abide in us (See John 15:5). This is the key to continuing fruitfulness, life, vitality, and power. He went on to point out, "Without me ye can do nothing" (John 15:5). We abide in Him as we get to know Him intimately through His Word. It is this that enables us to minister effectively, with power and authority.

Persistence Is Faith in Action

Jesus is the Light of the world, and when He comes into a person's life He dispels the spiritual darkness. This will last as long as the new believer continues to walk in the light of

127

God's Word. This requires consistency, constancy, commitment, and persistence. Persistence is a quality of living that refuses to give up. It will never say die. It will not yield to any opposing view or suggestion. It is relentless, unyielding, uncompromising, and radical. It is perseverance in the face of all opposition. It is a refusal to quit.

Persistence is a fruit of faith. In fact, it is closely related to faith. It operates according to the degree of faith that an individual possesses. The two blind men who followed Jesus demonstrated this quality of persistent faith. "And when Jesus departed thence, two blind men followed him, crying, and saying, Thou Son of David, have mercy on us. And when he was come into the house, the blind men came to him: and Jesus saith unto them, Believe ye that I am able to do this? They said unto him, 'Yea, Lord.' Then touched he their eyes, saying, According to your faith be it unto you" (Matt. 9:27-29).

Two blind men. They could not see, but they had heard about the power of Jesus. They were determined to find Him, because they believed not only that He could heal them but that He *would* heal them. Imagine what it must have been like for them. They could hear the crowds milling around the Savior, but they could not see Him. They did not have a seeing-eye dog to lead them to the Master. Apparently, they did not have anyone to show them where the Lord was. Yes, they had several obstacles to deal with. They could have chosen to grow discouraged. They might have said, "Oh well, it's no use. We'll never get to Him in this crowd. We might as well just go home and stay blind for the rest of our lives."

This was not their response, however. Their faith took control of their lives. Their attitude was, "He will heal us. I know He will heal us. We will not give up till we are healed."

Jesus loved them and He commended them for their persistence. Isn't it great that the first thing they saw after they were healed was Jesus. What an impression He must have made on them. They opened their eyes, and they saw Jesus. Before their healings, they had seen Jesus with the eyes of their spirits. They had accepted Him by faith.

In many ways we are like those two blind men. We cannot see Jesus either, but we know He is there and that He is able to do "exceedingly abundantly above all that we ask or think, according to the power that worketh in us" (Eph. 3:20). Jesus, in His love and mercy, has opened our eyes and now we can see. Like the anonymous blind men, we had to get through several obstacles in order to be healed and receive our sight, but we persevered and God rewarded our faith. He always does!

"According to your faith be it unto you," Jesus stated. That's the answer. If we believe for a little, we get a little. If we believe for much, we get much. We must be relentlessly persistent in order to make large strides in the spiritual realm. We cannot let anything stop us. We take hold of the answer we're looking for before we actually see it. We knock until the door is opened. We seek until we find. We ask until the answer comes. God rewards this persistently aggressive kind of faith.

The phrase "dogged determination" is useful in this discussion. A dog in the hunt is so determined to reach its goal that it is not aware of any obstacle in the way. He's no longer aware that he has fleas! He is not hungry, thirsty, tired, or discouraged. He is going to get his prey. He is going to perform for the master. This is dogged determination, and this is what is required in the life of every believer.

Sometimes we hear about dogs and cats that have been inadvertently separated from the families that love them. Often, these pets will traverse fantastic distances to return to their homes, to find their masters. There have even been stories of dogs that have traveled across country to find their former home. How does this happen? We could certainly say that such an animal has unbounding determination, and he refuses to be discouraged by anything until he reaches his goal. This, of course, is like the dogged determination that is required in the heart and life of the believer. It is an essential prerequisite to success in the Kingdom of God.

Though the dog might get hurt and beat up and get tired and hungry along the way, he adamantly refuses to stop his search. This has to be our stance as well. We must persist until our minds are renewed by the Word of God. God promises to renew our minds if we will stay in His Word, walk in His truth, and keep on keeping on. Countless Christians through the ages can testify that He has been faithful to His Word. You must keep your eyes on the prize. Set your face, as Jesus did, like a flint in the direction of all that God has for you. Remain single-minded in your pursuit of deliverance, healing, and transformation.

We keep on realigning our wills until they are congruent with the will of God as it is revealed in His Word. "And this is the confidence that we have in Him, that, if we ask anything according to His will, he heareth us: And if we know that He hears us, whatsoever we ask, we know that we have the petitions that we desired of him" (1 John 5:14-15).

We learn God's will by learning His Word. This process refuels us and builds us up in the "faith that was once delivered to the saints." It produces spiritual boldness in our lives. It makes us into radical followers of Jesus Christ. It enables us to call things into existence that don't exist in the natural realm.

One who is delivered from drug addiction is able, through this kind of faith and perseverance, to proclaim, "I'm a new creature in Christ. I'm filled with the Spirit of God. I have the mind of Christ."

This powerful approach sets people free from all sorts of addictions that have held them captive for years. It is for this reason that I am unable to support most secular programs that keep the person's addiction constantly in front of them. In many twelve-step recovery programs, for example, the former addict is required to confess, "My name is ——, I am an alcoholic . . ." This is the wrong kind of confession for a new creature in Christ to make. He or she is no longer an alcoholic, recovering or otherwise. He or she is no longer a drug addict, a homosexual, a shopaholic, a sex addict, a gambling addict, or anything else—if he or she has received Jesus Christ as Savior and Lord. Such a believer is a totally new creation in Christ Jesus.

When this faith-building process from the Word of God is set in motion in a believer's life, many unexpected things begin to happen. The cigarette smoker forgets his pack of smokes that had always been foremost in his mind previously. People in the midst of grief and mourning are surprised by a smile emerging on their faces. Depressed people become acquainted with joy. Those who were immersed in homosexuality discover an attraction to the opposite sex. Drug addicts find their inner emptiness filled by love. Gamblers become more interested in the numbers of hymns and Scriptures than the ones they used to bet. God changes lives. What He has done for others He will do for you.

A new life of victory, rewards, and freedom awaits all those who take the risk of crossing the bridge that leads out of darkness into light. It is a strong bridge that is paved with faith. Once across the bridge, people learn to exercise a faith that produces results. This encourages them to exercise even greater faith, leading to greater results. It's a wonderful place to be. That's why our Victory in Jesus meetings are filled with joy. The people who attend know that faith works. They know that Jesus is King. They know a God who loves to give miracles to His people.

Cross over the bridge that leads to life, happiness, results, and transformation. God will meet you on the other side.

7

Relentless Faith

*Therefore it is of faith, that it might be by
grace; to the end the promise might be sure to
all the seed; not to that only which is of the
law, but to that also which is of the faith of
Abraham; who is the father of us all.*
(Rom. 4:17)

By His Stripes You Are Healed!

A faith that works is a faith that prevails in all circumstances. This kind of faith reaps a harvest. The original Promise-Keeper (our Father in heaven) opens the windows of His storehouse and rewards our faith. "But without faith it is impossible to please Him, for he that comes to God must believe that *He* is, and that He is a rewarder of them that diligently seek *Him*" (Heb. 11:6).

Notice the importance of the word *diligently* in this context. This powerful adverb speaks volumes to our hearts about faith. It implies persistence (as we discussed in the preceding chapter), perseverance, and the relentless seeking of Him and His ways. The word "quit" does not exist in the vocabulary of Our Lord! Faith says, "I will not relent. I will keep on keeping on. I will persevere and make corrections until I learn how to pull the spiritual realm into this physical dimension and see the fruits of faith in this life." This kind of faith produces results because it is matured faith. It enables us to become promise-reapers in the Kingdom of God.

When we plant seeds of faith and cultivate the crop with the water of the Word of God, the sunlight of love, the power of faith, the plants grow and become very fruitful. So much so, in fact, that others can literally pick our fruit and go over the top with us. We rightfully expect, under these conditions, to reap a bountiful harvest. We've done our homework and our hearts are right before God, and this gives Him a green light to perform His mighty works in our lives because He's pleased by our faith in Him. This is the faith that is outlined in the Word of God, from Genesis to Revelation. This is the God-kind of faith, which is available to anyone who is truly relentless in diligently seeking the performer of His Word—God.

People need to see results. When faith begins to produce fruit in their lives they get encouraged. This process increases their faith level. Faith is not a matter of praying, "Increase my faith, Lord." Rather, it is standing on the promises of God's Word and believing that He will perform them no matter what the circumstances of life and this world might say to us. If you meet God's criteria, and are standing on His Word for you, then go for it! He will perform His Word.

Encouragement Leads to Inner Courage

Confidence in God builds as we see God moving in response to our faith. We know that we know that we know.

Others will tell us that we are foolish, but, thank God, He doesn't perform His Word based on what "they" believe and say. The devil will endeavor to lead us into doubt in an effort to defeat us (he loves to try our faith because he knows it works), but our relentless faith continues to say, "God is able to do anything but fail. He will do it for us. In fact He's doing it right now, He's bringing it to pass right now. As a matter of fact, He already has!" Relentless faith will thank Him for what He's doing right now and go into an expectancy mode, no matter what things may look like on the surface.

Faith begins as a seed, and it's your personal choice to cultivate it or not. If you choose to exercise faith in your life, you'll please God, and that very decision will increase your faith. God will show up by further encouraging you because you please Him. Like a fine French bread dough, your faith is folded over and over again. It is made of many delicate layers.

"(As it is written, I have made thee a father of many nations), before *Him* whom he believed, even God, who quickeneth the dead, and calleth those things which be not as though they were. Who against hope believed in hope, that he might become the father of many nations, according to that which was spoken, So shall thy seed be. And being not weak in faith, giving glory to God; And being fully persuaded that, what he had promised, he was able also to perform. And therefore it was imputed to him for righteousness. Now it was not written for his sake alone, that it was imputed to him; But for us also, to whom it shall be imputed, if we believe on Him that raised up Jesus our Lord from the dead; Who was delivered for our offenses, and was raised again for our justification" (Rom. 4:17-24).

Wow! The father of monotheism (belief in one God), Abraham, is the father of our faith. He believed God. He trusted His heavenly Father even though his natural mind seemed always to say, "No. It's foolish to think I'd have a child at 100 years old. It's impossible; it's futile." Abraham, according to some, would on the surface appear to be the most foolish man that walked the earth, but it was because of Abraham's faith that an entranceway was made into this earth for Jesus to come.

This happened because Abraham agreed with God for the performance of a promise. Abraham walked in faith. It was a relentless faith and it brought results. It enabled him and Sarah to have a child at an advanced age. It enabled him to become the father of many nations. It enabled him to have a family that was full of faith and blessing. All because he believed what God said. The beautiful part is that we are in his family! The promise is for us as well, "Now, we, brethren, as Isaac was, are the children of promise . . . For in Jesus Christ neither circumcision availeth anything nor uncircumcision, but faith which works by love" (Gal. 3:28 and Gal. 5:6). All we have to do is to appropriate the promise; that is, we must seize and lay claim to it, along with all the other promises of God's Word. All you have to do is commandeer your rights by reaching out for the promises of God in unrelenting faith.

Abraham was not weak in faith (and he didn't have Church history and the New Testament to strengthen him!), and we must not be either. If the doctor says, "It's over," believe God who says, "this shall not be unto death." In such a case, we must listen to God's words, not the doctor's. If science says, "It's impossible," trust God who says, "all things are possible to them that believe."

On numerous occasions we have had HIV-positive people attend our Victory in Jesus meetings. When they first come they are usually experiencing terror, waiting for the seemingly inevitable call of death that science says is coming to them. After being surrounded by our faith-filled services for a while, many of them find new hope, new life, a new purpose for living. It's beautiful to see them blossom from dying blooms to vibrant flowers in the garden of God's love. They are sustained by a faith that says, "By His stripes I am healed" (See Isa. 53:5 and 1 Pet. 3:24).

As they begin to see results, they are encouraged, and so are the rest of us. They believe God's Word and He rewards them with new hope, confidence, and stronger health. Their persistence and unrelenting faith pay off. They put their faith into action, remembering that "Faith without works is dead." They worked their faith and reaped faith-fruit from God. When this happens, their blood counts improve; they get stronger; and they start walking in newness of life. Sometimes their clinicians will ask, "Have you found some kind of cure for AIDS? We don't understand why you are improving so much?"

And they will answer, "Yes, Dr. Jesus. He never lost a case!"

The promises of God become so alive in them that they find it difficult to die when others think they're supposed to. When they find out that the terror they once walked with is a ruler of darkness who commands spirits of infirmity, they get angry and kick him out. When doubt creeps in, they tell that spirit to take a hike. And finally, some get so sharp at the battle that they forget about AIDS completely and use their new life to do one thing and one thing alone—to bring damage to the kingdom of Satan. They walk in faith. They walk in the Word. They walk in healing. They believe that God loves them and that nothing can tear them away from Him.

That kind of faith can't do anything but bring results. They don't feel sick anymore, and they don't look sick anymore. They don't focus on sickness anymore; instead they focus on the Giver of life whom they need more than life itself. All else must bow to the Lord of Glory!

Their spirits take over the place that was once ruled by their minds, and their minds are renewed by the washing of God's Word. They tell the doctors, "My God is able to keep me alive," then they simply keep forging ahead in their lives with the Holy Spirit, adamant, stubborn, and relentlessly refusing to go before their time. These former victims are not only happy, they are inexpressibly overjoyed over what God has done for them.

One young lady who came through Victory in Jesus meetings refuses to believe the doctor's diagnosis that she is infected with HIV. She doesn't tell others about the diagnosis, and she doesn't tell those that know about it that she is healed. Her reason for this is that she knows that many people will always try to throw her back into the old way of looking at her circumstances by asking, "How do you feel?" This is a natural response when we know someone is sick. She told me that she doesn't want to focus on her "feelings," because she knows they are an illusion. The true reality is spiritual, so she keeps on walking in faith, in healing, in trust. Her focus has completely changed.

Another lady, who became a member of Faith Fellowship, received ministry through Victory in Jesus for a personal problem she was experiencing. She found total victory through faith. Some months later she moved to Pennsylvania. When she discovered that her sister who was still living in New Jersey had been diagnosed with AIDS, she began to attend our meetings once more, driving all the way from Pennsylvania to central New Jersey—a distance of over 100 miles every Friday evening. She did so in order to keep her own faith level built up so that she could believe in behalf of her ailing sister. She was attending in proxy for her sister.

She would come to our meetings and the Lord would minister to her through the Word I preached in faith; then she would purchase our tapes and take them to her sister.

It wasn't long before she told us that her sister's blood count had gone up! She was listening to the tapes with her sister and reading the Word of God to her. The Lord was rewarding her faith. The sister who attended our meetings reported, "She's on fire for God, Brother Vinny!"

How do these things happen? God says that we are healed by the stripes of Jesus Christ on the cross of Calvary. We are healed. The doctors, the devil, society, and our families may say differently, but God says we are healed. We need to stand on His promise, take Him at His Word, and exercise full faith in Him. He always rewards such relentless faith by confirming His Word in people's lives and showing He is true. When we preach the Word, signs always follow: "And they went forth, and preached every where, the Lord working with them, and confirming the word with signs following" (Mark 16:20). This is happening today in Edison, New Jersey, and it can happen where you are as well.

God Is No Respecter of Persons

Though people often look at the outward appearance and the circumstances of others, God looks at our hearts. We're all the same before Him. He has no favorites. He does not look down on anyone. He loves us all.

How thankful I am that God is not like the people who judge and seek power over one another. He is a faithful Father who wants only the best for His children. People struggle with a variety of problems that result from the Fall of Adam. Sicknesses, addictions, fears, weaknesses, lust, discouragement, mental illnesses, depression, anxiety, etc. are manifestations of the kingdom of darkness in people's lives as a result of that Fall. This is why it is important for all people to enter the Kingdom of God and recover their rights. You do not have to clean up your act, as religion has told you. God will take you just the way you are because it's His desire to save all of us. God does not look upon a homosexual with hatred like many Christians and people of the world do. He doesn't look upon an HIV-positive individual with disdain as many human beings do. He looks upon all of us with love. He does not want to see any of us perish. The devil, on the other hand, seeks the destruction of us all. He tries to discourage us in a variety of ways.

A woman who lived in New York State began attending our Friday evening meetings because she was concerned about her brother who had an advanced case of AIDS. She told me, "Rev. Vinny, I'm coming with such a sense of persistence within. I'm building up spiritual confidence that I know will release the power of God in my brother's life. Because I know you are agreeing with me in prayer for him, I'm ready to go to the hospital and lay my hands upon his body. I have full faith that he will be healed. I feared doing this before I started attending Victory in Jesus, but now I'm ready to do that for which I've been prepared."

I sent her forth with the prayer of agreement as it is outlined in Matthew 18:18-29: "Verily I say unto you, Whatsoever ye shall bind on earth shall be bound in heaven: and whatsoever ye shall loose on earth shall be loosed in heaven. Again I say unto you, That if two of you shall agree on earth as touching anything that they shall ask, it shall be done for them of my Father which is in heaven. For, where two or three are gathered together in my name, there am I in the midst of them." We agreed in faith and God responded. He always does. He will never violate His promise to His children.

The lady from New York left our meeting, went to the hospital, laid hands of faith upon her brother, and he was healed. She believed he would be healed, and I joined my faith with hers. The man was healed! The power of God was released through faith, and the hospital discharged her brother. "Is there anything too difficult for the Lord?" (Gen. 18:14).

If Peter could say to a lame man that he didn't even know, "Silver and gold have I none, but such as I have give I thee; In the name of Jesus Christ of Nazareth rise up and walk" (Acts 3:6), how much more should we be able to exercise faith in behalf of our loved ones, members of our family, who have been trapped by the devil's devices? God wants you to use your faith in behalf of your loved ones. He is no respecter of persons; we're all equal in His eyes.

We're Out of Here!

Another very special lady who attended Victory in Jesus meetings was very concerned about her nephew, Angelo, who had taken an overdose of medication and was being treated at a nearby hospital. After a series of examinations and treatments, they discharged Angelo and sent him home.

Later that day, however, because of all the drugs he had taken, the hospital called back and left a disturbing message on the family's answering machine. "It is imperative for Angelo to get back to the hospital because the results of his blood work indicate he is in a life-threatening condition that could affect his heart. He must come back!"

Angelo asked his family to contact his aunt. When she got there, they decided to take him back to the hospital, but before she left with him she gathered the family for a time of prayer. They called down the stronghold of infirmity in the name of Jesus. They believed God.

Later, in the emergency room, the doctor examined Angelo and began to administer further tests. His aunt addressed the physician with a word of faith, "Look, here's the deal. Go ahead and do the tests you want to do, but make sure you're finished by 6:00, because at that time, whether you're finished or not, we're out of here! We serve a living God and tonight we have to go to church!"

Angelo and her aunt could see the health professionals snickering in response to her statement. They ran additional tests, and glory to God, they could not find a single problem with Angelo's heart. They tested and tested and tested, but they couldn't find anything wrong. What had appeared to be a death sentence fell dead at the feet of Jesus who is victorious over sickness and death. They pulled out of the hospital parking lot and pulled into the church parking lot, and God received the glory for a miracle that Angelo praises Him for to this day.

Angelo's aunt had relentless faith. She refused to listen to man's physical pronouncements and ran to God. She exercised her spiritual authority and took control. She began by going to the Lord in prayer, lifting up the matter to Him. (He always takes good care of His property!) Then she spoke faith to the disturbing situation and commanded it to go into darkness (where it belonged). She proceeded to make a statement of faith to the unbelievers in the hospital (who laughed at her). But God showed up, and He changed the situation. He proved himself to be real and powerful in response to her faith. It wasn't Angelo's faith that saved the day, but his aunt pulled down power from heaven in his behalf. Faith has substance. Faith wins. It believes in the seemingly impossible. It acts in accord with spiritual principles, not natural ones. Faith enables the power of God to be manifested in the physical realm. It brings heaven down to earth.

Only Believe

"And they came unto him, bringing one sick of the palsy, which was borne of four. And when they could not come nigh unto him for the press, they uncovered the roof where he was: and when they had broken it up, they let down the bed wherein the sick of the palsy lay. When Jesus saw their faith, he said unto the sick of the palsy. Son, thy sins are forgiven thee" (Mark 2:3-5). The Pharisees who were present (some are always around) began to quibble and judge. They thought it was blasphemous for a man to say that another's sin's were forgiven. Jesus, who knows all things, understood what they were thinking and murmuring about. He said, "Why reason ye these things in your hearts? Whether it is easier to say to the sick of the palsy, Thy sins are forgiven thee; or to say Arise, and take up thy bed, and walk? But that ye may know that the Son of man hath the power on earth to forgive sins, (he saith to the sick of the palsy), I say unto thee, arise, and take up thy bed, and go thy way into thine house. And immediately he arose, took up the bed, and went forth before them all; insomuch that they were all amazed, and glorified God, saying, We never saw it on this fashion" (Mark 2:8-12).

Jesus is the Great Physician. He healed all who were oppressed by the devil (See Acts 10:38). A man had the palsy. His four friends were concerned about him. They endeavored to take him to Jesus, but the throngs of people who surrounded Jesus prevented them from doing so. They made an opening in the roof of the house and lowered their ailing friend into the area in front of Jesus who was preaching to the crowds. Their persistence was an act of relentless faith, and Jesus took notice of it as He always does.

The paralyzed man's real need aroused compassion in the hearts of his believing friends, and on his behalf, they acted upon their faith in Jesus' power to heal. They were persistent and relentless as they tore through the roof. They refused to quit. This should be our response as well. When we know that someone we care about needs divine intervention in his/ her life, we should help them to get it, by responding in faith in their behalf.

We teach this at Victory in Jesus meetings. When those in attendance hear the Word preached and are liberated out of their own captivity, they are equipped to put their faith into action on behalf of those they love and care about. Oftentimes, they will bring their friends out of the darkness of this world into the Kingdom of God's love and light. They, in turn, then will find deliverance from all manner of sin. God sets them free. Each, in turn, brings others into the fold, and God gets all the glory. It's wonderful to be a part of something that works in such dramatic ways.

Jairus, one of the rulers of the synagogue in Jesus' day, had a daughter who appeared to be so sick that she was at death's door. He had heard about the Master and sought Him out with a tenacity that refused to quit and refused to believe that his daughter had to die. When he found Jesus, Jairus said, "My little daughter lieth at the point of death: I pray thee, come and lay hands on her, that she may be healed; and she shall live" (Mark 5:23). There wasn't an inkling of doubt in his heart. He believed God. He knew Jesus would heal his daughter and he acted upon his faith. His was not a weak faith that might say, "I know Jesus can heal her, but will He?" Instead, his faith was built on God's promises of healing.

Jesus agreed to go to Jairus' house. Along the way, He healed a woman who had been bleeding for twelve years because she had acted on her faith by touching Jesus' garment. Jesus said, "Daughter, thy faith has made thee whole" (Mark 5:34). In the meantime, however, Jairus' daughter had died and a household servant came to him to report the bad news. In effect, the servant said, "No need to trouble the Master any further. Your daughter has died."

It was the worst news Jairus could have received. Jesus heard what the servant said and responded to Jairus by saying, "Be not afraid. Only believe." I'm sure the man thought, "Believe what? It's over."

I can hear Jesus saying, "Believe what you originally believed, she shall live and I will do it." And Jesus confirmed His word to Jairus by continuing to go to his house and commanding the young girl to get up. She rose from the dead through the healing power of God which emanated from the spiritual realm into and through the physical vessel of Jesus. God is always faithful to confirm His Word to anyone who is in agreement with Him.

When Jesus said, "Jairus, be not afraid. Only believe," He bound the spirit of fear that was seeking to operate in Jairus—a fear that had the power to destroy his victory. In relentless faith, Jesus pulled the healing from the spiritual realm to the child. We are to walk in faith as our Master did. Jairus remained at the Master's side, even in the face of intensely bad news. He was persistent and unrelenting even though the devil tried to discourage him. Jairus took the victory!

This is what the Lord still says to us today as well, "Only believe."

Don't Listen to the Doubters

People in the world don't believe in miracles, and regrettably this is true of some people within the Body of Christ as well. It's for this reason that I encourage our people not to tell doubters about the miracles we experience on a weekly and daily basis. As a case in point, we had ministered to a homosexual man who exhibited many feminine characteristics. He walked like a girl and talked like a girl. He was delivered from his homosexual orientation by the power of God, but some of his feminine characteristics remained in evidence. A brother in the Lord came up to me and said, "If he has been delivered, why does he still act like a girl?" He was implying that the young man had not been delivered. He was planting seeds of discouragement and doubt, perhaps unknowingly, by way of a question that seemed perfectly natural.

That was the problem. The question was natural, not spiritual. The sower of doubt and discouragement was in the church, and he was looking at the other man's outward appearance, not at his heart. Outward appearances, as we said before, are merely representations of a person's spiritual condition. God is concerned with our spirits. I responded to the man's question with these words, "His mind is being renewed by the Word of God. Don't be looking at his outward appearance. Focus instead on what God's doing deep within his spirit. When his mind is renewed, his mannerisms will change. He will become fully the man God created him to be." And that's exactly what happened.

Don't listen to the naysayers. Listen to God. Watch out for the negative words and attitudes that crop up even in the church. Realize that God is a Spirit, and He works on the spirit of man first. Outward changes follow the inward work of His grace.

I believe this is why Jesus would often tell those He healed, "Don't tell anyone about your healing. Go to the priest." The priests were God's representatives to the people. They were not supposed to be discouraging others. People in the outside world, however, like the Pharisees, do not have faith for miracles and healings, because they are looking through the lens of the natural world instead of the spiritual realm. How can they believe until they first meet saving faith? If you're young in the Lord, it's probably better not to tell people about the miracles and healings you've received only in the sense that their doubtful responses can thwart you, distract you, and pull you back into the natural realm and its way of looking at things. Therefore, if the only way for you to "Be not afraid, Only believe," is for you to keep quiet, then this is what you must do, until you mature in the Lord and are grown up enough to handle it. The negative forces at work in the spirits and minds of those around us can actually steal a healing from us. When you are healed or receive another deliverance from the Lord, that's the time to steep yourself in the Word of God and refurnish your house.

Negativity, which is doubt, poisons your spirit. Get away from it. Don't listen to doubt. Keep on keeping on even if everyone around you expresses doubt. Enjoy your deliverance (your extrication from danger) instead. God will reward your faith walk. You will become a promise-reaper if you will only believe and keep on believing. All things are possible to them that believe.

Freely share your personal experiences in God with those who walk in faith, not by sight. They will support you. They will agree with you in prayer. Praise God for all He has done, is doing, and will do. Keep your eyes on Him.

Turn Your Eyes Upon Jesus

Jesus dispatched His disciples in a boat as He went up a mountain in order to pray. A tremendous tempest blew into the region, causing tremendous waves and winds that tossed the boat up and down in every direction. It was a frightening time (in the natural realm) for the disciples, and Jesus knew they needed a visit from the spiritual realm.

The Master went to His men, but He went to them by walking on the surface of the sea. He walked on it as if it was concrete. Being already frightened, when the disciples saw Him they were terrified. From all that we have learned thus far we know they definitely were not in a faith walk. The alarmed disciples saw something approaching the boat, and they thought they were seeing a ghost. Faith feeds faith. Fear feeds fear. As Jesus drew closer to them He said, "Be of good cheer, it is I: be not afraid" (Matt. 14:27).

Jesus was already battling. He knew He was in control of the spirit behind the raging elements. It was an interesting scenario—a bunch of scared men thinking they're seeing a ghost. Imagine their sense of surprise when they found out the "ghost" was their Teacher. The One who healed all who came to Him was walking on the water, and telling the disciples to "Be of good cheer."

This was a lesson for us all, but, it still hasn't gotten across to most people because I can count on one hand the people I know who can be of good cheer in the height of a raging storm. It isn't easy to do this. People who can be of good cheer in difficult circumstances are strong in faith, and they have learned how to live in the Sprit and walk in that domain. The winds and waves assail but they are not afraid. War clouds loom on the horizon but they do not despair. Diagnoses of death do not scare them either. They are not poisoned by doubt and fear.

Jesus wants to build our faith. When He asked Peter to get out of the boat and walk on the water too, Peter took a step out into the deep and entered the spiritual dimension with Jesus. Once he took his eyes off Jesus, however, his natural eyes were opened and he saw, water, winds, and waves. His spiritual eyes closed. Peter saw only the circumstances, the physical situation. This led him to think that walking on the water was an impossible task, and down he went! He went under. To Peter the sea had turned into a gigantic mixing bowl set at high speed instead of a walkway. The spirit of fear won and he cried, "Save me!" What had started out in faith had turned into a fiasco because Peter didn't keep his eyes focused on the Giver of supernatural abilities. Jesus stretched forth His hand to help him and rebuked him, "O thou of little faith, wherefore didst thou doubt?" The New Jersey translation being: "Why didn't you work the little faith you have into a larger portion instead of questioning whether you could do it or not?" (Matt 14:31).

Jesus was there for Peter as He is always there for us. All we have to do is to step out into the deep where He lives and then we can walk on the water with Him. Keep your eyes on the example of God's power—Jesus Christ risen from the dead—not on your inadequacies. Train your faith not to falter by taking little faith steps that increase the portion you were given at the new birth. If you fail along the way, reach for the Master's hand, but don't stop practicing. Work that faith deliberately and witness the power of God. You can never have too much faith!

If you are able to set a captive free, you do not have too much faith. If you pull prosperity down to a needy person, you do not have too much faith. If someone who was blind now sees, you do not have too much faith. If you turn the tide of government, you do not have too much faith. Jesus, the Giver, has more to give!

I once heard of a little girl who was sick. As she lay in her bed she looked at the mirror on the opposite wall that reflected a picture of Jesus that was hanging over the head of her bed. One afternoon her mother walked into her room and found her crying. "Why are you crying?" she asked the little girl.

The child responded, "Mommy, when I sat up in bed I couldn't see Jesus. I saw myself." The little girl had learned a profound lesson of life—every time we see ourselves we cannot see Jesus.

"Wherefore seeing we also are compassed about with so great a cloud of witnesses, let us lay aside every weight, and the sin which doth so easily beset us, and let us run with patience the race that is set before us, Looking unto Jesus the author and finisher of our faith; who for the joy that was set before him endured the cross, despising the shame, and is set down at the right hand of the throne of God" (Heb. 12:1-2).

8

True Liberty

Now the Lord is that Spirit: and where the Spirit
of the Lord is, there is liberty. But we
all, with open face beholding as in a glass the
glory of the Lord, are changed into
the same image from glory to glory, even as by
the Spirit of the Lord.

(2 Cor. 3:17-18)

The Real Thing

The devil immediately recognizes a phony. All too frequently we've seen people delivered from his snares for only awhile. Then they fall back into enemy hands. This is not necessary. If we will continue to walk in the Spirit, as Paul advises, we will not fulfill the lusts of the flesh (See Gal.5:16).

What often happens is that people get their eyes off Jesus. They begin to turn to other "gods" because they get weary of the fight of faith. They are looking for an easier way—perhaps a New Age philosophy, Transcendental Meditation, recovery programs, religious denominations, psychological therapies, self-help books, etc. These things look good, but they're not the real thing. They do not have the answers for the human spirit. These answers may have some good in them, but they are temporal.

There's a very fine line in the spiritual dimension between the supernatural (where God abides) and the emotions of the human soul. There's a vast difference between spiritual understanding and head knowledge. Though there may be some good and some truth in secular programs and approaches (and, to a lesser extent, other philosophies and religions), we must always recognize that emotional and intellectual approaches have no power to restore the human heart and soul.

Self-help is not the answer. We can help ourselves all we want, but what we really need is Spirit-help. The Spirit of God has power to restore, to redeem, to heal, to renew our spirit and soul. Any attempt we make toward self-improvement, if the Spirit of God is not involved, will end up only as self-improvement. We don't need an improved self. What we truly need is a *new self*—one that is fully alive to the Lord, transformed by the power of His Spirit.

Seek Help Where It Will Be Found

The spiritual realm has only one entrance. The sign above the door reads "Faith." Faith is the only way into the spiritual realm. There is no other way. It's the only way to victory. "For whatever is born of God overcometh the world: and this is the victory even our faith" (James 5:4).

Anyone who is not in tune with the Spirit of God cannot help you, no matter how well-intentioned he or she may be. The real need of our hearts is spiritual. A counselor, therapist, minister, teacher, psychiatrist, or other helping professional, unless empowered by the Spirit, can only work in the soulish realm of our emotions, will, and intellect.

The Word of God exemplifies this truth in several passages of the Old and New Testaments. In 1 Samuel 4, we have the account of Israel at war with the Philistines. During the first battle Israel had lost 4,000 men. All appearances indicated that the children of God were losing. They returned to camp with defeat clearly registered on their faces. They now expected to lose the battle, so their leaders had a meeting.

Like many of us are prone to do, they began to complain, express doubt, and blame God for their situation. Instead of expressing faith, they were confessing doubt, discouragement, defeat, and despair. This is the same choice that is available to each of us when difficult circumstances arise.

The Israelites did not check themselves to see if they were perhaps at fault in any way. They failed to acknowledge their own evil ways. Had they done so, they would have quickly discovered that they weren't serving God at all. Instead, they were serving their own selfish needs. Even their leaders lacked love for God. For example, the sons of the high priest were perverted.

In the face of this grim situation, they had a committee meeting. This is the best man can do. They didn't have a prayer meeting—they had a discussion. Someone has rightly quipped, "A camel is a racehorse that was put together by a committee!" It's the best the human mind can do—to come up with an idea and to try to implement it.

The Hebrew leaders decided to go to Shiloh in order to get the Ark of the Covenant so they could take it with them into the next battle. The Ark of the Covenant sheltered the presence of the Lord, a type of the Holy Spirit, the source of all spiritual power. This, they reasoned, would save them from their enemies.

They dispatched Eli's sons, Hopni and Phinehas, to get the Ark. They managed to do so, and as they brought the Ark of the Covenant back into the Israeli camp, a tremendous shout broke forth among the people. The Bible says that it was such a great shout that the ground shook and the "earth rang."

The rejoicing of the people resounded from the nearby hills and even the Philistines heard it. They must have known what had happened, because they knew about the Ark of God, and they were afraid of its power. They knew that Israel's battles with other enemies had been won successfully when the Ark went into battle with them. The Philistines grew afraid of defeat.

Israel's real enemy, however, was not just the Philistines. It was a spiritual enemy—the same enemy we face each day. Their spiritual enemy knew they were in sin and rebellion against God. This was Satan's opportunity to gain ground against them.

The Philistines were in such a state of panic that they decided to wage an all-out assault against their enemy. They did not want to end up as the Egyptians had. Their furious invasion, fueled by fear and frenzy, resulted in the deaths of more than 30,000 Israelis that day!

What happened? The Ark was there. Why didn't it save them? There was true power in the Ark, but they still lost the battle. How could such a thing happen?

It is one thing to be in the presence of God, but quite another to tap into His power. We can be in God's presence and still fail to avail ourselves of His strength. Sometimes we try to put God into a box of our own making, confining Him, instead of letting Him be the power of God unto salvation in any given situation.

The Jewish leaders thought that just having the Ark there would save them. They overlooked key issues of repentance,

154

faith, and obedience that are prerequisites to receiving the promises of God. Their earlier shouts of joy and victory came from their emotions, not their spirits. Despite their sin-infested situation, they thought God would deliver them if they simply carried the Ark of the Covenant into battle with them. This human idea did not work, because it was incomplete. There was truth in it, but they failed to understand how to apply the truth. The power of God was there to help them, but they failed to avail themselves of His power.

Their faith was in a material object, not in the God of the Covenant. The Ark was like a good-luck charm to them. Their answer looked good, but it was not real. Satan quickly recognizes a phony. He knows when our hearts are right with God. He fears us only when we are relying on the spiritual power of God. It was their spiritual emptiness that defeated them.

You Cannot Fool the Devil

The devil knows the difference between a true believer and a phony. The Bible points this out clearly to us in several passages. In Acts 19, for example, we read the story of the seven sons of Sceva. They had seen Paul performing miracles in the name of Jesus Christ and they wanted the same kind of power the apostle had demonstrated. They had seen him cast out demons in the name of Jesus. When they called upon the name of Jesus, however, nothing happened. Paul functioned in God's sector of the supernatural (over the natural dimension), but Sceva's sons acted out of their emotions and had no power over the natural realm.

Like the Israelites in battle, they thought that a certain ritual or form would give them power they needed, failing to understand that active faith in Jesus Christ is required in order to prevail in any situation. When the seven sons of

Sceva tried to cast out evil spirits, the spirit responded, "Jesus I know, Paul I know, but who are ye?" (Acts 19:15). Next, the man in whom the evil spirit was residing leaped on the sons of Sceva, overcame them, and prevailed against them. They had to flee from the house naked, wounded, and confused. The evil spirit had spotted these phonies and he was able to win the battle. The evil spirit was operating in the spiritual realm, and the seven sons of Sceva were functioning in the realm of the intellect and emotions. Therefore, they had absolutely no power against a spiritual force of wickedness.

The born-again believer who has turned his or her life over to Jesus Christ is a helpless infant until he or she is fed with the milk of God's Word, had his or her mind renewed, and is delivered from bondage in every area of life.

In the U. S. Army, a new recruit is not sent into battle until he is equipped, trained, and renewed in his thinking. The same is true in the spiritual realm. The child of God needs to grow up and become real and strong in the Spirit before the enemy will recognize him or her as a real threat.

The mature Christian who knows the truth of God's Word, stands upon His promises, and relies on the Spirit, is able to bring down spiritual strongholds, take back lost territory, overcome all obstacles, and prevail in every battle. Such a believer can release the power of God, calling out evil spirits that seek to harm human beings.

Be sure you're "for real" before you try, like the seven sons of Sceva did, to call out the evil spirits. Grow in the Lord. Demonic spirits can come against and oppress you if you're fooling around with something you are not prepared to handle. Get equipped to do battle and become all the Lord says you are so that you will be able to recognize spiritual attacks and become proficient enough to launch a counterattack. If you think you can fool any spiritual power, you're wrong. You can't fool Satan, and you can't fool God. Sometimes you may be able to fool people around you, and even yourself, but you can't fool those who live in the spiritual realm.

Develop your spirit life and your spirit walk. This will bridge the gap between your thoughts and God's thoughts—your ways and His ways. Be sure to be ready before you go into battle. Get the proper equipment (See Eph. 6), and be trained in the things of God (See 2 Tim. 2:15; 3:15-17), and stay prayed up (See 1 Thess. 5:16-23).

If you try to engage in *real* spiritual warfare before you are ready to do so, you might end up being the casualty. You may look good and sound good, but unless you are prepared, you are headed for trouble. You cannot fool your enemy. The Israelites fooled themselves and the Philistines, but they did not fool Satan, so they lost. Without true discernemnt in spiritual warfare, you will be shooting in the dark. Someone who shoots in the dark can easily injure themselves or someone they love.

Spiritual attacks come to God's people whether they're equipped to battle or not equipped to battle. Make a decision to learn how to battle, and then fight to win.

If you are living and walking in the Spirit you will be walking in the light. You will recognize the enemy and he will recognize you. The power of God will be your protection and your weapon. You will win every time. You will be a constant threat to the enemy, and he will not hang around because he will be too busy trying to recuperate from your last victory. Be subject to God. Resist the devil and he will flee from you," (James 4:7). These are marching orders from the Lord!

Where Are the Prophets?

Those in leadership have to face a temptation that those who are not in leadership may not be aware of. The temptation is to surround ourselves with "yes-men," people who will tell us what we want to hear. Usually such "yes-men" are afraid to take a stand against their leader.

This is what happened when Ahab was the King of Israel. In 1 Kings 22 we read that Jehoshaphat (of Judah) was visiting Ahab (of Israel.) They agreed to join their forces together to reclaim territory they had lost to the Syrians. Jehoshaphat suggested that they ask the Lord how to proceed.

Ahab then called for his 400 prophets to give them counsel. These "prophets" did not know the true God. They were heathens. Ahab inquired of them, " Should we attack the Syrians?"

All 400 responded that Ahab's idea was a good plan. They chorused, "Go!"

Jehoshaphat, on the other hand, was still not certain it was a good idea. He asked, "Ahab, isn't there a prophet of the Lord here in Israel?" Somehow he knew that the other prophets had said what sounded good and even looked good, but he sensed that it was not the real thing. In fact, it was a lie.

Every leader's success depends totally on his walk with God and the counsel around him which he chooses to listen to. Every leader needs counselors who will tell him what he *needs* to hear, not necessarily what he *wants* to hear. The former counsel may be a true life-saver in many situations whereas the latter kind always leads to defeat. Ahab had 400 men around him who were useless, they told him what he wanted to hear because they were afraid of losing his favor.

A single prophet, who was unafraid, told the king what he needed to hear. This prophet advised him not to go into battle. The prophet's name was Micaiah. Ahab did not want to hear this man's counsel. He said, "There is yet one man, Micaiah the son of Imlah, by whom we may inquire of the Lord: but I hate him, for he doth not prophesy good concerning me, but evil" (1 Kings 22:8). Ahab hated the prophet of the Lord because he would not tell him what he wanted to hear.

Rather, Micaiah was a true prophet who said, "As the Lord liveth, what the Lord saith unto me, that will I speak" (1 Kings 22:14). The truth may sometimes seem to hurt *for the present,* but it has the ultimate power to set us free and preserve life. "And ye shall know the truth, and the truth shall make you free" (John 8:32). "If the Son therefore shall make you free, ye shall be free indeed" (John 8:36).

A true prophet's counsel is truth. His prophecies come true. But Ahab had the ability to persuade. He was the King of Israel, so there was a covenant relationship between him and Jehoshaphat. To make matters worse, they were related by marriage, so the peer pressure was heavy on Jehoshaphat, so he gave in and went to war. In the case of Ahab, who neglected to heed the Lord's counsel, his pride led to a mortal wound in battle. Jehoshaphat managed to escape death by the grace of God only because he was smart enough to cry out to the Lord. The ungodly cannot call the shots for the godly. It simply will not work.

We Receive From Faith by Using Faith

It grieves me to see the battlefield littered with casualties of spiritual warfare. Some of the wounded ones never get up again. The recovery of others sometimes takes a long time.

Such was the case with a woman named Christine who began attending Victory in Jesus meetings.

She had been saved a few years earlier as she watched a TV ministry. Through this means she enlisted for service in the army of the Lord. She thought she was ready for warfare. She was a "lone ranger" who never attended church, however, and she failed to stay in the Word. To make matters worse, she didn't know how to pray. Clearly, she was an easy target for the devil's shooting practice.

The first thing that happened was that her husband was injured in an automobile accident. Though he got saved, he was stabbed soon after that, then developed spinal meningitis and died! This all happened in the short space of two years, and it left Christine a total wreck.

Christine had been healed by the Lord, both spiritually and physically, and she had faith for her husband's healing as well, but he felt he wasn't good enough to be healed. They didn't know that the Word of God was there for them to stand firmly upon. Therefore, they did not know how to release spiritual power in the battle. They didn't even know they were in a battle, so the devil won that round.

Soon after her husband's death, Christine began attending church at Faith Fellowship where she learned about Victory in Jesus. She began attending our meetings faithfully. She describes her experience as follows: "I came into Victory in Jesus on a stretcher of grief. I had gotten carried off the battlefield as a casualty of war, but it wasn't long before I had to go to war again.

The next time the battle concerned my eighty-nine-year-old father. He was going through congestive heart failure. This time was different though. I got agreement in prayer, which Rev. Vinny emphasizes in Victory in Jesus meetings. That prayer sent a new heart to my dad. I was learning, so I said, what the heck, I'll send him new lungs, too! My sister and I laid hands on him in agreement against the doctor's bad report, and the power of God canceled the doctor's words. We never mentioned the words 'congestive heart failure' again. It was a fight, but my dad was discharged from the hospital."

It was a joy to see Christine growing in the grace and the knowledge of the Lord. Her faith was dynamic and radical. It was a relentless faith that often comes to someone who has experienced great suffering.

She went on, "I went back to Victory in Jesus and continued to grow and learn. A year later something similar happened. This time my father had a stroke, but I was a year older in the Lord. As I was sitting in the 'jump-seat' of the ambulance, I told the paramedic that I was just going to sit there and pray. He said that he thought that was a good idea. The power of God came upon me in the ambulance and I leaped to my feet, placed my hand on dad's head, and said, 'I come against you in the name of Jesus. Loose my father!' Then I sat down.

"When we arrived at Overlook Hospital's emergency room they took my father into a room for treatment. While he was in there I had to remain at the desk to give the nurses the necessary information that is required for treatment. The next thing I knew the paramedic who had agreed with me about praying for my father had placed his two hands on my shoulders and said, 'You got your miracle. Go in and see your father and the two doctors who are standing there with their mouths open!'

"Dad hadn't even been admitted, and yet his whole left side had straightened out, including his face which had been distorted by the stroke. They decided to keep him for observation and tests, but he was soon discharged. His doctor said, 'That's really unusual for a ninety-year-old!' The best thing about his hospital stay was that his medications were reduced to almost nothing. Now he is ninety-two-years old and he is gardening!

"It took me awhile to understand what had happened to me. One day I caught myself laughing and dancing and singing praises to God, and it was only seven months after my husband had gone to be with the Lord. I remembered how it had taken me ten years to get over my mother's death. Finally I understood. I had gone into the battlefield, but I didn't have any bullets to fire at the enemy. I had been shooting at the enemy with an unloaded weapon! Now I can face the enemy, and face him I must, with ammunition from the Word of God, and when I pull the trigger of faith, I release God's power by speaking His Word over any situation. God's Word of faith is in me now. Once I speak it, I rest in the arms of my heavenly Father and watch Him destroy the enemy instead of Him watching me get slaughtered over and over again. That's the protection He wanted me to have, and I praise Him for it."

Christine uses her faith to get much from the Lord.

A Bullet-Proof Uniform

God has clothing for you and me to wear. He speaks of His armor in Ephesians 6. He wants us to wear the helmet of salvation, the loincloth of truth, the breastplate of righteousness, the shoes of the gospel of peace, the shield of faith, and the sword of the Spirit. He wants us to put on each piece daily with prayer.

He also commands us to be clothed with the garments of salvation and the robe of righteousness (See Isa. 61:10). The Lord wants us to be clothed with humility as well. (See 1 Pet. 5:5).

God tells us to put on incorruption and immortality (See 1 Cor. 15:53-54). He expects us to wear Christ as our "protective shield" (See Gal. 3:27). Paul writes, "And that ye put on the new man, which after God is created in righteousness and true holiness" (Eph. 4:24). He further explains,". . . put on the new man, which is renewed in knowledge after the image of him that created him" (Col. 3:10). This "new man," Paul points out, is one who has "Put on therefore, as the elect of God, holy and beloved, bowels of mercies, kindness, humbleness of mind, meekness, longsuffering,; Forbearing one another, and forgiving one another, if any man have a quarrel against any: even as Christ forgave you, so also do ye. And above all things put on charity; which is the bond of perfectness" (Col. 3:12-14).

Our uniform as believers, therefore, is incomplete if we are not wearing Christ Jesus, His salvation, righteousness, faith, love, mercy, truth, the Word, peace, humility, immortality, holiness, kindness, meekness, patience, and forgiveness. Without these items of apparel, we are naked when we go out to confront the enemy.

How do we obtain this uniform? It is through the Word of God and the Holy Spirit. In fact, most of these qualities are listed in Paul's famous dissertation regarding the fruit of the Spirit. "But the fruit of the Spirit is love, joy, peace, longsuffering, gentleness, goodness, faith, meekness, temperance: against such there is no law" (Gal. 5:22-23). We are commanded to "be filled with the Spirit" (Eph.5:18).

Whenever you see someone acting in faith you have no trouble discerning the uniform they are wearing. You don't have to ask yourself, "Whose army are they in?" You immediately recognize whose side they're on. Their actions give them away.

Once we make the choice to follow Jesus as our Commander-in-Chief we are sent to boot camp to learn the basic principles of the Word of God. We are trained to be rooted in His Word and to take our stand upon it. We learn how to use His Word as the sword of the Spirit. This all-important training does not take place overnight. It involves stages of growth and practice and discipline. Through our training we learn how to act and how to keep our uniform neat, well-pressed, and shiny.

Our training prepares us for battle. It sharpens us up. It gives us the stamina we will need. This is what we endeavor to do with each new recruit at Victory in Jesus. We prepare them for battle with the enemy.

The First Battle Is With Yourself

Every believer knows that the first battle that must be waged is the one that takes place within us. Very often it comes in the form of the discipline that is required to begin the diligent study of God's Word. This is a battle against a lazy, whining flesh that says, "I don't have the time," or "I don't feel like reading, or it's too hard to understand God's Word." That's the first battle we need to win. It involves our thoughts, beliefs, values, philosophies, and ideals. The battlefield is our mind.

When you give your heart to Jesus, and you begin to taste the spiritual freedom He provides, a fierce battle begins to rage. It does not involve flesh and blood, and it does not involve carnal weapons. It's a spiritual battle, as Paul points out, "For we wrestle not with flesh and blood, but against principalities, against powers, against the rulers of darkness of this world, against spiritual wickedness in high places" (Eph. 6:12). We must never forget this. Even though we cannot see the

164

principalities, powers, and rulers of darkness, they are very real and they see us. We have to fight them.

The Lord says you will win the battle if you fight in the way He outlines in His Word. In fact, you cannot lose because He has already won it for you. However, you must fight it with Him, in His way, with His weapons, while wearing the uniform He has given to you or you will lose.

It's important to realize, at the outset, that the enemy that you cannot see is going to attack your mind with thoughts you can't see. At first, you will think that these thoughts are your thoughts and they will deeply trouble and disturb you. The battle is unfamiliar to you, and you may think you're going crazy!

It's your first time in the fray. Through this initial experience you learn to discern the difference between God's thoughts, your thoughts, and the devil's thoughts. It takes practice, but you will learn. God's thoughts are revealed in His Word—your battle manual. The devil's thoughts are those which are contrary to the Word of God. Isn't it foolish to go to war without studying the instruction manual?

Once you learn this distinction, you will be able to regain control of your mind. You will win the battle. As you gain victory in battle after battle you will win the war because you will learn to fight with the spiritual weapons God has provided for you. You will win.

The Battle for Your Will

The next battle you will face is the battle for your will— that part of your soul that makes decisions, choices, and commitments. The devil doesn't want you to will God's will. He doesn't want you to choose to follow Jesus or to commit your life to Him. He will hit you with thoughts like, "It's too cold, rainy, early, or late to go to church." He will do everything He can to prevent you from growing in God.

You exercised your free will when you chose to follow Jesus in the first place. Your will is the choice-maker. Imagine a car that belongs to you. Let's assume that your will is in the driver's seat. Let's say that the car is your mind. The vehicle will idle pointlessly if the driver fails to step on the accelerator. It will careen dangerously if the driver does not steer it. It will remain motionless if the driver does not start the engine. That's exactly the way it is with our minds and wills. They both need to be renewed.

All our lives, until we became believers, our minds controlled us. The human mind always seeks to be in control. When your spirit is made alive to God, however, the mind loses its control over your life and will. Your new man is controlled by the spirit-man. Your will made a choice.

When the spirit-man takes control of "the car," as directed by the will, the mind becomes subordinate, going in whatever direction the spirit demands. This provides a smooth ride that reaches the intended destination every time even though it may encounter obstacles along the way. It is so much better than the old way, when the mind was in control. When the mind sits in the driver's seat, it is as if the car had been hot-wired, taking off and following the desires of the flesh.

Why does this happen when the mind is in control? Paul gives us the answer. "For I know that in me (that is, in my flesh) dwelleth no good thing: for to will is present with me, but how to perform that which is good I find not. For the good that I would I do not: but the evil which I would not, that I do" (Rom. 7:18-19). This is what happens when the mind is in control rather than the spirit.

Being born again is a spiritual process that is ongoing. Jesus saves you and delivers you so that you will not have to be a slave to sin and Satan any longer. You have escaped from the enemy's territory through the power of God. The fact that the devil has lost makes him very angry indeed, and this is why you experience so many battles along the way.

One night I received a call at home from a young man who had recently been born again. He was crying in his drunken state and he said, " Before I received Jesus I was a happy drunk, now I'm a miserable drunk!"

It was immediately clear to me that I had been woken up by an alcoholic spirit that had the audacity to get me out of a sound sleep! In righteous anger, I screamed into the receiver, "I command you to come out of him in the name of Jesus!" My shouting woke up my wife who was startled until she realized that I was overcoming the enemy in the young man's life.

The voice of my caller softened and I could sense a spiritual peace being restored to him. He began to speak clearly and soberly. Though he had been born again and saved, he was battling with his flesh that has no good thing in it.

We must remember that the flesh is under the law of sin. Through this understanding, we can realize that the former alcoholic will still crave liquor. The desire is still within his flesh. The same is true with any addiction. The person's flesh is so accustomed to whatever the compelling addiction is that it will battle for control of his or her life.

The young man was in a real battle. He had tasted freedom but his flesh was pulling him back into bondage. His will, that had chosen to follow Jesus and had formerly been in the driver's seat, had given in to his mind. This does not mean that he was lost, it simply showed that he was battling. His mind, unlike his spirit, would permit his body to drink.

This is where spiritual training in the Word of God comes in. It is absolutely necessary. Without it, the long ingrained habit patterns and responses will regain their foothold in the flesh. The mind has to be renewed with the Word of God in order to reverse life-long ways of coping and dealing with the stresses of life.

The Apostle Paul said, ". . . the will is present with me; but how to perform that which is good I find not" (Rom 7:18). This is normal. The good is found in Jesus, where He dwells by His Spirit in our inner man. We have no good in our flesh. All of our righteousness is as filthy rags in the sight of God. Without Jesus we can do no good thing. Through Him, however, we can do all things (Phil. 4:13).

When the will taps into the spirit, we find the power to do the good that we want to do. This happens as our mind is renewed by the Word of God. "And be renewed in the spirit of your mind" (Eph. 4:23). It was good for the young man to stop his drinking for all sorts of reasons, but he did not seem to have the power to conquer this addiction even after he gave his heart and life to Jesus.

The Double-Minded Man Is Unstable

Before the young man became a Christian he had been single-minded. The bottle contained his "answer," and he turned to it whenever troubles arose. When he became a Christian, though, he started being double-minded. When he was born again, the alcoholic spirit had to depart the premises of his life because Jesus had come in. Before this transformation took place, the unclean spirit of alcohol had found a home in him. That spirit had literally possessed him. When the idea of taking a drink to soothe his mind came to him, he had no defense against it whatsoever. He was powerless over his addiction. When his flesh wanted a drink, his spirit agreed. There was no disunity—spirit, mind, and body were in total agreement. Not so when he became a Christian, however. Now he was truly unstable in all his ways. (See James 1:8).

168

Before becoming a believer, the young man had problems, but he was single-minded in his response to those problems. He would simply turn to the bottle time and time again. One day in the future, he realized, he might die from his alcoholism, but that was some time in the far distant future, and he wasn't going to let it bother him *now*. This is true single-mindedness.

We need to be exactly that same way when it comes to the spiritual battles we face. We need to be single-minded in our faith. This is the way to win the battles. A mind that is single focuses on Jesus, His Word, and the power of God's Spirit. A double mind is tossed to and fro by every wind of doctrine. It is like the waves of the sea. Even someone who wants to do good, to overcome an addiction, cannot do so if his or her mind is double.

A double mind sidetracks an individual from acting upon truth. It blocks a person from knowing true spiritual freedom in the Lord. It prevents one from using the substance that faith provides in place of the substance that formerly had them under its control. A double-minded person is easily distracted and thrown off-course.

We need to stir ourselves up to take hold of the promises of God as Peter points out, ". . . stir up your pure minds by way of remembrance: That ye may be mindful of the words which were spoken before by the holy prophets . . ."(2 Pet. 3:7). Being mindful of the Word of God describes a mind that is full of the Word of God. This is a renewed mind— a single mind.

A defeated believer is one who has accepted Christ at an evangelistic meeting or as a result of personal evangelism and stopped there. He or she did not get in the Word, pray, fellowship, or grow. Sometimes such a person believes he or she has arrived when, in fact, they've only begun the battle. The enemy knows what's going on in their lives, so he moves back in when their defenses are down.

God has set us free to enjoy our freedom. He has declared war against the enemy of our souls. Jesus, His Son, lost His blood in this spiritual battle. Those who choose to remain defeated by allowing themselves to become entangled with bondage again are those who fail to be trained in the things of God. This gives the devil a field day in their lives. He shoots at them with any bullets he can find—disease, doubt, addiction, fear, anxiety, guilt, etc.

We need to know the seriousness of the battle. We need to face it with spiritual training and weapons. We need to walk in victory instead of defeat. Fighting the good fight of faith is not a matter of war dances—it's an out-and-out-war. The authority of God's Word always prevails.

"Stand fast therefore in the liberty wherewith Christ hath made us free, and be not entangled again with the yoke of bondage" (Gal 5:1). This is true liberty.

9

Trophies of Grace and Faith

Wherefore seeing we also are compassed
about with so great a cloud of witnesses,
let us lay aside every weight, and the
sin which doth so easily best us,
and let us run with patience the race that is set
before us. Looking unto Jesus
the author and finisher of our faith: Who
for the joy that was set before Him endured the
cross, despising the shame, and is set down at the
right hand of the throne of God.
(Heb. 12:1-2)

Faith's Hall of Fame

Most believers are familiar with the men and women of faith that are listed in Hebrews 11. This passage has often been called Faith's Hall of Fame, and it includes such notables as Abel, Enoch, Noah, Abraham, Sarah, Isaac, Jacob, Joseph, Moses, Joshua, Rahab, Gideon, Samson, and many who are not named. In this chapter, I would like to submit the names of some of the people Nancy and I have been privileged to work with; these modern believers, like the patri-archs of old, also deserve membership in Faith's Hall of Fame.

Their stories will bless your heart as you learn that each of these folks is like the men and women listed by the writer of Hebrews. Each one, ". . . if they had been mindful of that country from whence they came out, they might have had opportunity to have returned. But now they desire a better country, that is, and heavenly: wherefore God is not ashamed to be called their God: for He hath prepared for them a city" (Heb. 11:15-16).

All true believers have been set free from their captivity from the kingdom of darkness. We have been translated into the Kingdom of Light. The bondage of Egypt is behind us and we've entered the Promised Land. God is not ashamed to be called our God, and He has prepared a city for us.

God's Irresistible Power

Hope is one person who found victory in Jesus. She writes, "I had been tormented by the unclean spirit all my life. Even after I got saved and filled with the Holy Ghost, spoke in tongues, and experienced many personal physical healings, several areas of my life still haunted me."

This is a common experience of believers from all walks of life until they learn to see that the ruling spirit that has controlled their lives for so many years must be dethroned and replaced by theWord of God and the Spirit of God.

At a time of desperation in her life, Hope ran to God. He was there for her as James points out, " Draw nigh to God and He will draw nigh to you" (James 4:8). Sometimes we end the verse right there instead of reading on : " Cleanse your hands, ye sinners; and purify your hearts, ye double-minded" (James 4:8).

This is the true need of every believer once we have drawn nigh to God— we must cleanse our hands and purify our hearts. This is the process that keeps us from being double-minded, which James warns against, "A double-minded man is unstable in all his ways" (James 1:8).

The cleansing and purifying come through continual washing in the water of the Word of God. This gives us the faith we need to be overcomers and it renews our minds completely.

Thank God, Hope learned about this process before it was too late for her. She explains, "Repentance was never fully explained to me. I had my eyes on man (not on the Lord), and I soaked in a renegade doctrine which took the power of God out of His Word. This added insult to my injuries. I was totally unaware of the unclean spirit and familiar spirits that Satan had enlisted to work against me. Totally unaware!"

By "unclean spirit " here, I refer to the ruling spirit—the one in charge. The term does not necessarily have anything to do with sexual immorality, but it refers to uncleanness in the sense of spiritual impurity in its multifarious forms.

For many years, Hope, like so many others, went along in life without any effective power to win the battles she faced. She had been saved, filled with the Holy Spirit, and delivered of some besetting sins, but she was not truly victorious. She reports that she often thought, "I'm never going to make it. I must just be bad seed."

Hope and her husband, Tim, began to attend Faith Fellowship in Edison, New Jersey, in 1992. It had been twenty years since her initial conversion experience. Two decades of ineffective Christian living had left her powerless and almost hopeless.

For so many years it had seemed as if every time she took one step forward she would slide ten steps backward! She sensed that she had a call on her life, but she felt she could not fully arrive at what God had called her to be.

Through the ministry of Faith Fellowship and Victory in Jesus, Hope was able to find the answer that she had been searching for—for more than two decades. She writes, "When I heard Vinny Longo teach about the unclean spirit [See chapter 5], I couldn't believe what I was hearing. I listened intently and soon discovered that he backed up everything he was saying with the Word of God."

She went on, "All I had ever learned about the Lord started to come into focus. I began to hear the Word by faith and I learned how to keep Satan from stealing the Word from me. I learned about God's faith and the fruit-of-the-Spirit faith, and my walk with God took on new meaning. I learned how to speak the Word by faith."

It was wonderful to see Hope grow in faith. This did not mean, however, that all her problems were over. She wasn't in heaven yet. She writes, " I might add that at this time the persecution started to come on me in ways I never anticipated. Family members, finances, health, etc. I had made Satan mad, and he was out to discourage me!"

Always before, Hope had fallen prey to his devices. What made the difference now? It was faith. She learned to recognize the enemy's voice. She now knew how to take authority over him by standing on the Word of God. She puts it this way, "Jesus had taught this to me a long time before, but now I was starting to enforce it."

It made all the difference in the world. We must never forget that Satan is organized. He has a "computer print-out" concerning each child of God.   He is familiar with our weaknesses and our struggles.   Hope states, " He is out to kill us and if he can't take us to hell with him. He will endeavor to destroy God's purpose in our lives. This is serious stuff and it's no time for the army of God to go to war without knowing who our enemy is. We've heard about the armor, and we've heard about resisting in faith. Now let's find out who this enemy of the living God is, and let's make him our Lord's footstool."

Wise words from a woman who learned who her enemy is and how to deal effectively with him. As I read her words, I'm reminded of the earlier chapters of our book. Hope is exactly right—if we don't know our enemy, we'll never win the war! We must be ever-vigilant.

Hope describes the warfare this way: "Most of the Body of Christ doesn't even know we're in a war! If we are going to take nations for King Jesus, we will need an army equipped with the knowledge of their enemy, because that is the only way he will be defeated."

It is as I often say, we need to learn how to use God's irresistible faith, to speak God's irresistible words, so that God's irresistible power may be released.

"Fear, " Hope points out, "calls Satan to the scene, but faith calls Jesus to the scene."

Many times the unclean spirit comes upon us at an early age. This happens due to a multiplicity of factors, mostly in the form of hurts we've sustained while growing up. Sometimes these hurts are in the form of abuse, mis-understanding, persecution, abandonment, neglect, unfairness, and other problems. These provide an entrance into our spirits for the unclean spirit to take possession.

One young woman I know of is the victim of eating disorders; she lives in fear of eating! I'm quite certain that she doesn't really know who her enemy is. I believe this unclean spirit came upon her at an early age in response to certain fears, hurts, and insecurities.

Thank God, we don't have to live in the fears that stem from those early hurts. Each of us, like Hope and her husband, Tim, can rise above the hurts by taking authority over the enemy. This requires a violent kind of faith that takes hold of God's irresistible power.

From Crack to the Cross

Another person whose name deserves to be in Faith's Hall of Fame is David, who was delivered from wine and drugs. We thank God for David and for his inspiring testimony of the power of faith.

David has shared, "I know the hand of God has always been on my life. I just had to believe, receive it, and allow it to have its way in my life."

We all know that this is easier said than done, but by applying the principles of God's Word to his life, David learned how to walk in faith. His background, in many respects, had worked against him. He grew up in a public housing project as the youngest of seven children. His parents were strong disciplinarians, so David had a healthy respect for law and order. Nonetheless, his environment led him astray.

David explains it this way: "I was never prone to do bad things. Part of this was due to the promise of a spanking from my parents who did not spare the rod on us when we did something wrong, but I also had an instinct to stay away from trouble. This is not to say that I was trouble-free. On the contrary, when I was fourteen years old I got drunk on New Year's Eve. By the time I was sixteen I had become a full-blown hoodlum. As I look back on those years, however, I always seemed to stand out in the group as the one who was most afraid to steal or fight or participate in illegal activities. I know that the hand of God was on my life even then, steering me down paths of righteousness for His names' sake."

It sounds as if some guardian angels were watching out for David as well. That first experience with drinking when he was fourteen years old opened the door to a string of addictions in David's life. His friends led him to pot smoking, but he never got involved in pushing or selling drugs. Truly, the hand of God was on David's life even thought he didn't know it at the time.

He was sent to Vietnam by Uncle Sam. While there, the pot smoking continued on a regular basis. Next, he went to college where the drug use continued as he began to experiment with cocaine. He nearly lost control of his life at this point and came very close to being kicked out of school, but once more the hand of God protected him. He became the first member of his family to graduate from college in spite of his drug addiction.

God was watching out for David, but still he had no personal knowledge of Jesus or the Word of God. He went on to graduate school, where the use of drugs continued. Eventually, he dropped out because the addiction was beginning to be very serious and it worked against him greatly. God was good to David, and He provided a job for him.

Meanwhile, his younger sister accepted Jesus Christ as her personal Savior, and she began to pray for David. She led her brother in a prayer of salvation, which he followed with words after her but still failed to make Jesus the Lord of his life. David states his experience in these words: "I remained under the influence of the kingdom of darkness for several years after that time. It was during this time that I began using crack cocaine. The Bible teaches us we all have a cross to bear, and, believe me, crack cocaine was mine."

Soon thereafter, David found his way to Victory in Jesus, where he found deliverance from his addiction. He reports, "I had gotten to a point where my wife and children were pleading with me to stop using drugs and to get into a secular program, when God first filled me with His Holy Spirit, with the evidence of speaking in unknown tongues, and then began depositing His truths in me by leading me to attend Victory in Jesus meetings. I can remember getting so excited about the Word that came forth in Victory in Jesus that I was inspired to volunteer my time to help out with the ministry. I began by simply putting things away after the meeting, and God has since given me additional responsibility in the ministry producing letters, doing monthly reports, and counseling new believers on the meaning of salvation. God has delivered me from the powers of darkness and caused me to continue thirsting after His Word. Today you will find me at the back of the room at most Victory in Jesus meetings, giving praises unto our Lord and serving God's people.

And how thankful we are for David's service, his dynamic testimony, and his radiant faith. David never stopped thirsting for God's Word. Today he battles on the front lines, a trained soldier of the Lord. The Lord has filled him with spiritual discernment and a loving spirit, the fruits of the meat of the Word of God. From crack cocaine to the cross, this man of God has found that Jesus is the answer to his every need.

He sums it up this way, "The Victory in Jesus ministry has taught me how to grab hold of the things of God and to take authority over any of the enemy's attacks. I have come to realize that, through the teachings of Victory in Jesus meetings, God is my source, and no weapon formed against me can prosper. I know that I will always be learning more about who God is, and who I am in God, and I look forward to continuing my life in Him."

David has learned an important truth: "No weapon that is formed against thee shall prosper; and every tongue that shall rise against thee in judgment thou shalt condemn. This is the heritage of the servants of the Lord, and their righteousness is of Me, saith the Lord" (Isa. 54:17).

Standing Strong in the Lord

Eva, like David, struggled with drug addictions through much of her life. She began this horrendous journey at the age of fourteen when she started using qualudes and other pills. As time passed, she began to experiment with pot, mescaline, and LSD. She graduated to needles when she was seventeen. Her heroin addiction was followed by methadone maintenance treatment. For many years she was in and out of various treatment programs.

She was on methadone therapy for eleven years, and during that time she developed cancer. The cancer was a lymphoma that metastasized into the bones. The chemotherapy treatment caused her to lose all of her hair, and she had to have a hysterectomy.

All the trauma to her body necessitated the use of a shunt in her head in order to draw fluid and to receive chemotherapy. Through all of this ordeal, she had to face pneumonia several times and even had a bout with spinal meningitis. Eventually she was placed on various kinds of antidepressants.

Eva wrote about her experience as follows: "They said I was manic-depressive, which I now know was demons. After three years of chemotherapy, I went into remission. This took place in 1980. After that time, I continued on drugs even more. I got into many car accidents when I was high, and my life was threatened on several occasions. I even started using cocaine with the methadone, along with Valium, other pills, and alcohol.

"On November 28, 1985, I was totally delivered from the drugs miraculously. Since that time, at least 100 of my old friends have died. Many of them died from AIDS. In 1987, I developed gall bladder problems. They wanted to remove my gall bladder, but I refused the surgery and signed out of the hospital. Even though I had excruciating pain, I knew the Lord would heal me. I trusted in Him implicitly, and He rewarded me with a miraculous healing. I was also delivered from cigarettes.

"By attending Victory in Jesus meetings, I was able to learn how to stand on God's Word. I learned how to remain strong in the Lord. Now, I'm totally free!"

Eva, like David, Hope, and myself, learned to ". . . lay aside every weight, and the sin which doth so easily beset us, and to "run with patience the race that is set before us." She is now "looking unto Jesus the author and finisher of our faith," and she is a blessing to everyone who meets her. She has found the ultimate high in Jesus, her Lord and Savior—her mighty Deliverer.

It Didn't Go Off!

Carl is another beautiful trophy of God's grace and love. He started using drugs when he was fifteen years of age. He was in high school at the time, and was a very good student. He graduated in the top quarter of his class and went on to college, where he hoped to get a very good education. The devil had other plans for him, however.

As a successful high school athlete, Carl reasoned it would be good for him to play football in college. When he tried out for the team, his coach remarked about his natural ability for the sport and soon put him on the first string. He became something of a "big man on campus," and this led to many temptations that Carl had not anticipated—and that he was far from prepared to face. He had grown up in an Islamic home and knew absolutely nothing about Jesus or the promises of God's Word.

Carl tells us what happened next: "I didn't study or pray or anything. And Satan came in like a flood! I quickly became absorbed in the drugs and women that were freely offered to me at school. I didn't go to class and my grades became a joke. I didn't care about anything but getting high and partying. I soon lost my place on the team as well as being dismissed from school. So I went out to live on the street.

" I soon became a drug dealer and collector. I lived and worked in New York City as well as various parts of New Jersey. I carried a gun, but to the Lord's glory, I never used it. However, I did have a stand-off with a drug 'customer' in which we both held guns at each other. Both of us backed down, however, and soon after that incident I left the 'family,' as the drug ring had called itself.

"From there on my life spiraled downward to the point where I was running a crack-house in my hometown of Plainfield, New Jersey. I stole and did many other things to support my habit. I was even threatened by a 'customer' that came to the crack-house who didn't like me. He told me that he would shoot me if I didn't give him some crack. He then pulled out a sawed-off shotgun, pointed it at my chest and pulled the trigger! I heard the firing pin hit against the shell and go, 'Click.' The gun had misfired!

"During all of this time there was another fellow who had been recently saved and who had been telling me about all that Jesus did for him. He kept asking me to come to Victory in Jesus. After the shotgun misfired, though, it didn't take me long to go."

The night Carl showed up at Victory in Jesus he came up to the prayer line. He saw others falling under the power of God. That's when he made up his mind and told himself, "I'm going to stand firm on my feet." So he planted his feet firmly on the ground and took a linebacker's stance, and the next thing he saw was the violence with which the unclean spirit threw him to the floor as he slid up the aisle. When he got up, however, he was completely free! Carl had experienced a total delivery from drugs and alcohol. He has not experienced so much as even a desire for them since that meeting to this day.

God broke through to Carl by using a true life-threatening experience to get his attention. This frequently happens to those who have lost all sense of right and wrong through their addictions. Clearly, someone who loved Carl more than he loved himself had protected him, because that Someone had a plan and purpose for his life.

Carl had gone to several secular treatment programs, but to no avail. He was living in what he described as "a revolving-door-world of going to programs, getting out, then within a week going back to the drugs. I was possessed by a drug-addicted spirit and I didn't know it."

It has been more than six years since that time and Carl remains drug-free. Jesus has set him free.

He gladly proclaims, "Today I am living an overcoming life in Jesus. I have been blessed with a beautiful wife, two blessed and wonderful children, a new home, and a business. I am also now on the staff of Victory in Jesus, overseeing the staff, counseling the newly delivered, and sharing my testimony of how God gave me the victory. It is my prayer that this testimony will show to anyone who reads it that our God is willing and able to do anything."

Victory in Jesus - a Reality

These trophies of grace point out to us that there is victory in Jesus. This is a reality. It is true. It is vital.

Jesus said, "But now I go my way to him that sent me; and none of you asketh me wither goest thou? But because I have said these things unto you, sorrow hath filled your heart. Nevertheless, I tell you the truth. . . ." (John 16:5-7). Jesus always agreed with reality. His disciples, however, did not want to agree with the reality that Jesus had to leave them in order to pursue a higher purpose. They wanted him to remain with them always, so they avoided the truth. They wanted to stay in denial so they engaged in wishful thinking, hoping that the words of Jesus would somehow go away. They were compromising with truth.

Unlike those disciples, however, Hope, David, and Carl— three of our trophies of grace—have decided to agree with reality. This means that they agreed with the truth. Jesus said, " I am the way, the truth, and the life: no man cometh unto the Father, but by me" (John 14:6). Jesus is the truth. There is no other way.

Our Lord explains it further: "If ye continue in my word, then are ye my disciples indeed; And ye shall know the truth, and the truth shall make you free" (John 8:31-32). The key to spiritual freedom is knowing the Truth (Jesus) and continuing in His Word. Any other approach to freedom will fail, even if there is some truth in it. Jesus said it best, "If the Son therefore shall make you free, ye shall be free indeed" (John 8:36).

A young woman named Elaine explained this process in a poem she entitled "Ultimate High." The last three stanzas show us what happened when she acknowledged Jesus as her

Deliverer. (Remember, He is far more than simply a "higher power," He is all power in heaven and on earth!) Her inspiring verses are as follows:

> I took the needle, threw it out and said,
> "Now I'm free indeed"
> I know now this is Jesus and
> He'll supply every need!
>
> I said, "Jesus is Lord, God raised Him
> from the dead," and
> repented for all my sin.
> I instantly felt a warm glow,
> And some kind of change within.
>
> I knew the Lord had surely touched me,
> and I began to cry.
> All these years of my life wasted,
> I've finally reached my Ultimate High!

The Uncompromised Word of God

Truth, as we have discovered in these pages, is the uncompromised Word of God. It involves believing the Word of God, and having confidence in the Word of God.

As you act on the Word of God, the Holy Spirit will guide you into all truth, as Jesus promises: "Howbeit when He, the Spirit of truth, is come, he will guide you into all truth; for he shall not speak of himself; but whatsoever he shall hear, that shall he speak: and he will shew you things to come" (John 16:13).

God's Holy Spirit is the Spirit of Truth. He lives within us and it is He who makes the Word become a part of you. The world cannot receive the Spirit of Truth, but every believer can: "And I will pray the Father, and he shall give you another Comforter, that he may abide with you for ever; Even the Spirit of truth, whom the world cannot receive, because it seeth him not, neither knoweth him, but ye know him for he dwelleth with you, and shall be in you" (John 14:16-17).

The Spirit and the Word are one, and through faith they shall be with you and in you. This is the key to victory in Jesus, because it involves agreement with His truth. There is no compromise when our lives are "hidden with Christ in God" (Col. 3:3). This is the secret to victory that the trophies of grace in our chapter have found, and you can find it too !

Godly Sorrow

There are two kinds of sorrow in life—godly sorrow and worldly sorrow. One leads to repentance and the other leads to death. Paul writes, "Now I rejoice, not that ye were made sorry, but that ye sorrowed to repentance: for ye were made sorry after a godly manner, that ye might receive damage by us in nothing. For godly sorrow worketh repentance to salvation not to be repented of: but the sorrow of the world worketh death" (2 Cor. 7:9-10).

Worldly sorrow is rooted in the sinking sands of human sentimentality. It has no power, only feelings, and we all know that human feelings are fleeting, changeable, and fickle. Godly sorrow, on the other hand, leads to life because it shows the human heart its need for repentance.

Repentance is the first true act of faith. We believe on the Lord Jesus when we hear His Gospel. The Word produces this faith in our hearts. It's enough faith to reach out and take the Master's hand. In order to do so we must be earnestly sorry for our sins and make a commitment to walk away from them, to walk by faith and not by sight. When we do so we are repenting. It is the goodness of God that leads us to repentance in the first place (See Rom. 2:4).

His grace and His goodness enable us to be saved. "For by grace are ye saved through faith; and that not of yourselves: It is the gift if God: Not of works, lest any man boast" (Eph. 2:8-9).

Notice the role of faith in this process. Faith begins with the Word: "But what saith it? The word is nigh thee, even in thy mouth, and in thy heart: that is, the word of faith, which we preach; That if thou shalt confess with thy mouth the Lord Jesus, and shalt believe in thine heart that God hath raised him from the dead, thou shalt be saved. For with the heart man believed unto righteousness; and with the mouth confession is made unto salvation. For the scripture saith, Whosoever beleiveth on him shall not be ashamed" (Rom. 10:8-11).

Godly sorrow leads us to repentance. We need to be sorry for our sins, our wrong choices, our wasted years, our failings, and all the rest. This is the first step toward change, a response of faith to the Word of God that each of our trophies of grace have taken and continued to walk in.

The Word of God changes our lives. "For the word of God is quick, and powerful, and sharper than any two-edged sword, piercing even to the dividing asunder of soul and spirit, and of the joints and marrow, and is a discerner of the thoughts and intents of the heart" (Heb. 4:12). By immersing ourselves in the Word daily, we are able to stand strong in faith. By speaking the Word, we are able to overcome. It is our weapon, our light, our transformer, our power, and our guide.

Walking in the Word brings victory in Jesus.

10

New Creations in Christ

Therefore if any man be in Christ, he
is a new creature:
old things are passed away; behold, all
things have become new.

(2 Cor. 5:17)

Spiritual Gifts

Paul writes, " But the manifestation of the Spirit is given to every man to profit withal. For to one is given by the Spirit the word of wisdom; to another the word of knowledge by the same Spirit; To another faith by the same Spirit; to another the gifts of healing by the same Spirit; To another the working of miracles, to another prophecy; to another discerning of spirits, to another divers kinds of tongues; to another the interpretation of tongues; But all these worketh that one and the selfsame Spirit, dividing to every man severally as he will" (1 Cor. 12:7-11).

We thank God that each of the gifts of the Spirit have been in operation in our Victory in Jesus meetings. Without these gifts we would have made little progress.

The word of wisdom and the word of knowledge are continually present as we share the Word of God with one another. The gift of faith comes to us in response to our hearing the Word. The prophetic ministry comes forth in preaching, teaching, and timely messages from the heart of God. Tongues and their interpretation bring edification to the Body of Christ. By way of the gift of discerning of spirits, the Holy Spirit reveals the presence of other spirits or a human spirit not of God.   The Holy Spirit is the only discerner of hearts (spirits), and we are dependant upon His guidance in these matters.

The strong man's strategy, however, is a fact of life. The unclean spirits lust after human beings in a desire to control us.   The unclean spirit yields only to a higher authority. The commands issued by a child of God, operating in this higher authority in the name of Jesus, are the means that defeat the strongman (unclean spirit). The Word of God repeated by a child of God activates spiritual authority, which is in compliance to heavenly rank and file as authorized by Jesus, our Lord and Savior.

This leaves us with the remaining two gifts of the Spirit: healing and miracles. There is a notable distinction between the two. From our experience, the gift of healing begins a process of restoration in the life of the people we work with; it may or may not be an instantaneous healing, however. Usually it is a process that takes place in the individual's life over an extended period of time.

The gift of miracles, on the other hand, is clearly in operation when a person is miraculously restored to health and wholeness in an instant of time. This happened in the life of a man named Raymond, who is now a pastor in Virginia. Raymond had been an alcoholic for fifteen years. His wife began to attend Faith Fellowship, and she shared with us about her husband's problem with strong drink.

A staff member called Raymond and invited him to attend Victory in Jesus meetings. He agreed to do so, but in his mind he determined that he would "fool God." Prior to the meeting, Raymond bought a pint of liquor and polished off half of it. His wife realized what was happening so she said, "If you don't go to church tonight, you can pack your bags."

Considering the alternative, Raymond decided he would follow his wife's advice. He went to a Victory in Jesus service and went forward for prayer for salvation. As I ministered to this troubled man, I was almost overcome by the stench of alcohol on his breath. Nonetheless, I prayed for him and commanded the unclean spirit to come out of him. From that moment on, Raymond was set free from alcohol, and I noticed that even his breath changed. There was no detectable odor of alcohol left. This was the gift of miracles in operation.

Raymond never again craved alcohol. Instead, he craved Jesus. All desire to drink had left him. Literally overnight, he became a Christian who was on fire for God. He attended every class and service offered by the church, including two years of Bible school and ministry training. He eventually joined the staff of Victory in Jesus.

Other people receive the gift of healing, but their process of restoration may take longer. We always give an invitation to receive Jesus as Savior at our meetings. When Raymond, like so many others, came forward, I laid hands on him and commanded the unclean spirit to leave his body. I ordered it never to return. I took authority over the situation in his life in the name of Jesus. Raymond's first response was uncontrollable crying as God did a totally miraculous work in his life.

Raymond is now the pastor of Faith Fellowship in Suffolk, Virginia. He has a weekly radio program that he calls "Victory in Jesus." Anyone who hears Raymond minister the Gospel hears God's love and compassion, the ever-present touch of God that this man received and held onto since the day the shackles of death were broken off his life by God. He can teach about victory, because he has experienced it in full measure.

Plant Seeds of Faith

Our job as believers is to plant seeds of faith in people's hearts whenever we can. We are sowers of the Word. Jesus said, " A sower went out to sow his seed: and as he sowed, some fell by the wayside; and it was trodden down, and the fowls of the air devoured it. And some fell upon a rock; and as soon as it was sprung up, it withered away, because it lacked moisture. And some fell among thorns; and the thorns sprang up with it, and choked it. And other fell on good ground, and sprang up, and bare fruit an hundredfold. And when he had said these things, he cried, He that hath ears to hear, let him hear. And his disciples asked him, saying, What might this parable be? And he said, Unto you it is given to know the mysteries of the kingdom of God; but to others in parables, that seeing they might not see, and hearing they might not understand. Now the parable is this: The seed is the Word of God. Those by the wayside are those that hear; then cometh the devil, and taketh away the word out of their hearts, lest they should believe and be saved. They on the rock are they, which when they hear, receive the word with joy; and these have no root, which for a while believe, and in time of temptation fall away. And that which fell among the thorns are they, which, when they have heard, go forth, and are choked with cares of riches and pleasures of this life, and bring no fruit to perfection. But that on the good ground are they, which in an honest and good heart, having heard the word, keep it, and bring forth fruit with patience" (Luke 8:5-15).

Our job is to sow the seed (the Word of God). When a farmer sows seed, he does not reach down, dig it up, examine it, and put it back in the ground. He simply waits for God, through nature, to bring forth fruit. In the meantime, the farmer tries to make sure that the seed is cultivated properly, well-watered, and free from entanglement with weeds and other factors that can choke life from the seed.

At Victory in Jesus, Nancy and I have seen all three kinds of people—those who refuse the Word of God, those who receive it eagerly at first and then fall away, and those who receive the Word readily and keep it from then on. Naturally, the latter category is the one we like best. These are people who, like Raymond, stay on track from the moment they receive God's Word.

Others, however, do not take root. They believe for a while, but when temptation comes their way, they succumb. We work with people like this as well. We teach them, nurture them, love them, and pray for them. We endeavor to lead them to refurbish their "houses" with the Word of God once the unclean spirit has been cast out.

Recruited, Not Born That Way

We live in an age when much attention is given to homosexuality as an "alternative life-style." This euphemism for an age-old sin implies that the sexual orientation is a matter of personal choice even though "gay rights" advocates would try to tell us that homosexuals are born that way. Some will even say, "God made me like this."

191

Our experience in Victory in Jesus meetings has revealed that homosexuals are not born that way. Rather, they have been recruited by other homosexuals, captives to the same spiritual stronghold. Unbeknownst to them, these people have been actively sought out by unclean spirits and many of these were subject to and taken captive by perverse sexual assaults in their youth.

By engaging in homosexual acts, the individual unwittingly opens the door to the strongman, the homosexual ruler spirit that seeks to dominate them.

Many homosexuals, both male and female, have found deliverance at our meetings. The unclean spirit is kicked out of their house, but he seeks to reenter. The strong man attacks the person in the flesh, but the real battle takes place in his or her mind. The unclean spirit previously had control of the individual, and so he seeks to regain the territory he has lost through evil thoughts. He seeks to direct the former homosexual back to the natural way of looking at things. He wants the person to think, "I was born that way. It's no use. I am a homosexual. It will never change."

In fact, the enemy uses this same tactic no matter how the person was taken captive. Persons who are freed from drugs may be offered "free drugs," the next day. It makes no difference what the bondage was, the enemy wants the person back. This is the reason I always emphasize at Victory in Jesus that the battle is fierce and real. We're fighting a supernatural war with a real enemy. That's why everyone needs to come to know their God or they will be defeated by a no-holds-barred killer. That's why we fight, through the Lord.

At Victory in Jesus I've had numerous experiences in which homosexuals have come forward for prayer. They wait in line, then stand in front of me. The first time an unclean homosexual spirit within a man spoke to me I was taken back. When I approached the man to pray for him, the unclean spirit confronted me with these words, "You can't have him!" I stepped back, startled, as I discerned what was taking place. I thank God, who in that split-second, counseled me by showing me how He handled a similar incident. In a flash, He brought to my mind a picture of the time when He was confronted with these same spirits. He simply commanded, "Peace, be still!" The Lord spoke to me, *That's how I handled it, Vinny; be yourself.* With this rhema knowledge, I stepped back into the fight and said, "Shut up, and come out of him in Jesus' name." The words spewed out of my mouth with power, and the unclean spirit had to obey the spiritual authority that came forth under the command of Jesus Christ. He had no alternative but to obey. The spirit immediately vacated the premises, but before he did so, he threw the man violently to the floor. Why did my simple command work? Because we have the spiritual authority and power of Christ within us. When we tell the unclean spirits to leave, they must obey us.

People fall into the pit of homosexuality because they are recruited by unclean spirits who seek to make more homosexuals, knowing that in this way they will destroy a large segment of God's creation before they ever find out what their purpose on earth is. The evil spirits want a miserable early death for these homosexuals.

The hope for the lesbian, the hope for the homosexual, in fact, the hope of the entire world is found in the Son of God, Jesus, who offers a renewed mind by the Spirit of God and His inspired Word. There is no other hope.

We knew of one lesbian who experienced this change in a radical way and now she is a woman of unrelenting faith in God, who is rewarded daily for her faith. At first, the change was not outwardly detectable. She still had a man's haircut and a light beard. She spoke with a raspy, almost masculine voice. But when she came under the authority of the Word of God, her inner man experienced dramatic changes. She felt differently, thought differently, and believed differently. Her spirit began to change first, and then her outward appearance began to change as well. Eventually, she let her hair grow longer. Her clothing was more feminine, and her voice was more like an alto's than a baritone's. She began to look like the beautiful woman God had created her to be. She renounced her former life-style. The enemy had tried to make her think she was more like a man than a woman. It was a bald-faced lie from the pit of hell. Now she is a beautiful woman of God, a handmaiden of the Lord. Her skin is smooth; there's not a trace of a beard; her face is pretty; and her voice sings the songs of God with the beauty of a soprano.

God is able to do exceedingly, abundantly above all that we can ask or think (See Eph. 3:20). All we have to do is to stand upon His promises, to act upon His faith, to believe His Word. The result will be a form of relentless faith that cannot fail. This is God's will for you and for me, and He will bring it to pass if we will let Him. Glory be to God!

God says, "Thou shalt not lie with mankind, as with womankind: it is abomination" (Lev. 18:22). The homosexual faces a fierce battle when he or she is born again. The same is true of any long-term life-style bondage. The good news is that it's a winnable battle. Anyone who states anything other than this states a lie. The new creation is a reality, not just a combination of words.

Some homosexuals have come to our meetings when they are still living with their same-sex lovers. When they go home, therefore, they are immediately faced with temptation even though they now claim Christ as their Savior. We don't tell homosexuals who come to Christ what to do; rather, we preach the Gospel. We take our authority in the spiritual realm, by praying for these individuals, and we are confident that God will begin to show them what to do.

In most cases that involve homosexuals, the healing is a process rather than an instantaneous miracle. One former homosexual we had the privilege of working with is Jim. He was saved at one of our meetings and then continued to attend Victory in Jesus services on a fairly regular basis. When he was saved he was living with a male lover.

We prayed for Jim, asking God to guide his life. We taught him to stand fast in the liberty God had given to him. A couple of months later, Jim came to talk to me. He said,

"Brother Vinny, I've just moved out of the apartment I was sharing with my friend," he told me. Now I have my own apartment. A lot of women have been saying how pretty my blue eyes are, and I've been able to respond to them honestly by saying how pretty they are."

"Jim," I advised, "stay cool in that area too."

This young man is now married to a beautiful Christian lady. His healing was not an instantaneous miracle, but it was a miracle nonetheless. The majority of homosexuals we work with, male and female, have to go through a process of healing in order to *manifest physical changes*.

The first time I was confronted with this issue at our Victory in Jesus meetings I was reminded of Paul's words: "And such were some of you: but ye are washed, but ye are sanctified, but ye are justified in the name of the Lord

Jesus, and by the Spirit of our God" (1 Cor. 6:11). Despite what the world, psychology, science, social workers, and others might say, I know it is possible for a homosexual to find deliverance in Christ.

God cannot fail. He is ". . . able to do exceedingly abundantly above all that we ask or think, according to the power that worketh in us" (Eph. 3:20). The enemy wants homosexuals to believe that their situation is hopeless, but the Word of God tells a different story. No one is hopeless from God's point of view. He wants all of us to be saved, delivered, and healed. He is no respecter of persons. Jesus came to save the lost.

Unclean spirits don't have any right to manifest themselves in the physical realm. They are spiritual creatures, and they have no authorized right to manifest in the earthly realm. The earth was given to the man, Adam, and it was spiritually reclaimed by the Son of Man, the second Adam, Jesus. In seeking to embody a person without permission, that is, to use the physical body of a human being by instilling their thoughts into a human mind in order to carry out their will on the earth, they seek to be able to perform in the affairs of man. This is so, because when a person begins to entertain and lay claim to the unclean spirit's thoughts he, unknowingly, gives a destructive spiritual power a place (a house) from which he can operate. Soon thereafter, that person will begin verbalizing those thoughts, and when they are spoken they begin to come into fruition. Therefore, it is the natural man that gives unclean spirits the privilege and the power to speak and act in the earth.

We must always remember that the only power the enemy has is the power we give him. This is why demonic spirits look for weaknesses in the flesh, a place from which they can exercise control. They are constantly seeking an open door from which they can operate. Simply put, as we stated before, in chapters 4 and 5, they want to control and to destroy.

Paul knew this from a personal experience, and, therefore, he urges us all to "Walk in the Spirit, and ye shall not fulfill the lust of the flesh" (Gal 5:16). The pride of life, the lust of the eyes, and the lust of the flesh have been open doors in people's lives for the entrance of unclean spirits. The human mind is their playground.

Walking in the Spirit

Walking in the Spirit is not an automatic process that takes place when a person is born again. It takes time, discipline, study, practice, and experience in order to effect such a walk in each of our lives. Nevertheless, we must begin this all-important walk or suffer the consequences. At Victory in Jesus, we urge people who are delivered to keep coming back until their minds have been renewed by the Word of God and they have faith to walk in the Spirit on an ongoing, daily basis. Anything short of this is, we realize, spiritual suicide.

Walking in the Spirit involves standing fast in spiritual freedom. Paul wrote, "Stand fast therefore in the liberty wherewith Christ hath made you free, and be not entangled again with the yoke of bondage" (Gal. 5:1). Once you gain ground don't give it up again. Go forward from there. It is our responsibility (our response to His ability) to maintain all the territory we conquer. We maintain our deliverance by walking in the Spirit and walking in the freedom we have been given. If we fail to do so, we will get entangled with the yoke of bondage that previously held us back.

We exhort each one who comes to us to learn about who they are in the Spirit. Individuals come with all sorts of problems, but we teach them what the Word of God states about who they are in the spiritual dimension. We train them to take their thoughts captive. With this knowledge they can fight winning battles. We teach them to take the sword of the Spirit (His Word) and couple that with the Lord's strategy so that they can pierce their enemy to death instead of becoming embroiled in a bloody massacre of the flesh, which only wounds the enemy, at best, and leaves the person totally disillusioned with the power of God.

As the believers progress, they come to the understanding that nothing is achieved in the physical world unless it is achieved in the spiritual world first—and that nothing is achieved at all without faith. Our training at Victory in Jesus always begins with the principles of God's spiritual dimension. This is so that each individual can begin living in the Spirit. We teach them where that spiritual realm exists, what occurs in that dimension, what their position is in that domain, and how they may effectively live in that territory so that they may be able to continuously walk in it and live a life of victory.

This information is vital because it's impossible to continuously live in an area that we know nothing about, much less walk in it. "If we live in the Spirit, let us also walk in the Spirit" (Gal. 5:25).

We tell homosexuals, lesbians, and all who come to us, that they need to walk in the Spirit and the Lord's gift of freedom in order to avoid fulfilling the lusts of the flesh. They are held accountable to God, who is ever ready to help them to forsake their former ways. God says, "Let the wicked forsake his way, and the unrighteous man his thoughts: and let him return unto the Lord, and he will have mercy upon him; and to our God, for he will abundantly pardon" (Isa. 55:7). This is true for homosexuals, drug addicts, child molesters, wife beaters, the mentally ill, the murmurer, the proud, and everyone else. We are wicked without God. We need to forsake our evil ways and thoughts. We need to return unto the Lord. When we do this in unrelenting faith, God will have mercy on us—and He will abundantly pardon us.

This is the good news of the Gospel of Jesus Christ. If we come to the Lord willingly and follow His ways, He rewards us. If we maintain our rebellion and our sinful ways and choose to go against God, we suffer the consequences of that choice as well. God will not violate our free will, the gift He gave us to enable us to make the right choice.

Jesus is the hope of freedom for homosexuals as He is for everyone. God knows what is good for us. It is not His desire to make life miserable for anyone. Our enemy is doing that. He doesn't get joy out of punishing us. He wept for His people at Jerusalem. As a matter of fact, He wants us all to find abundant life and unspeakable joy. These spiritual blessings cannot be found in the lusts of the flesh, be they homosexual or heterosexual. There is no good thing in our flesh.

God gives people up when they change His truth into a lie. The New Testament bears this out: "Wherefore God also gave them up to uncleanness through the lusts of their own hearts, to dishonor their own bodies between themselves: Who changed the truth of God into a lie, and worshipped and served the creature more than the Creator, who is blessed forever. Amen. For this cause God gave them up unto vile affections . . ." (Rom. 1:24-26).

God loves His creation, which includes all of the captives. He wants to rescue homosexuals because He loves them; what He hates is their sin. God makes it clear to all of us that, if we pursue a course that deviates from His plan and purpose, we will end up with "no good thing."

Good and Evil Are Accountable to God

In the ancient Book of Job, God reveals much about our adversary—the fallen angel of light. In chapter one, the Lord exacts an answer from Satan. " Now there was a day when the sons of God came to present themselves before the Lord, and satan also came among them. And the Lord said to satan, From where did you come from? Then satan answered the Lord. From going to and from on the earth and from walking up and down on it" (Job 1:6-7). This account shows us that the entire angelic creation, powers of good and powers of evil, are both accountable to the Lord God. When God's authority demands an answer from the evil one, that answer must come forth.

We have learned much from Jesus' example in the New Testament. He shows us how to deal with Satan and his evil agents because of their destructive intentions toward mankind. Through Jesus' ministry, we learn that satanic power always needs embodiment. The unclean spirit needs a human body to use.

Therefore, no matter what the presenting problem in a person's life is, we know that the ruler has found a body that he can subjugate, control, and operate from. When we hear of mass murders and child killers, we know an unclean spirit is at work. In fact, all we have to do is watch the news to see what the unclean spirits have accomplished that day.

A different administration, but the same operation of an unclean spirit, is in effect in the lives of drug addicts, homosexuals, alcoholics, pedophiles, voyeurs, exhibitionists, prostitutes, gamblers, smokers, the envious and jealous, murderers, creators of strife, deceivers, the treacherous, backbiters, gossipers, slanderers, and others (See Romans 1: 29-30). The goal is one and the same, the total destruction of a human being.

As believers operating in God's authority, we need to remember that good and evil spirits are accountable to us. When we commission angels, we expect good events to follow our spoken words, and when we confront evil, we expect the unclean spirit to obey us. When we give orders to leave to an unclean spirit, he has to leave. This is the only way the enemy's house can be divided. A child of God must order it so in the name of Jesus. The power of attorney has been handed over to the children of the Kingdom by Jesus, and they must use it.

Through this teaching, enslaved individuals begin to understand that there is hope for them. They do not have to be beat up forever. They can beat up the enemy themselves for a change. In fact, it's their right to do so! They can experience and have true victory in Jesus.

A successful lawyer came to one of our meetings. He had been undergoing treatment for manic-depressive disorder for several years. As a matter of fact, he was spending more than $200.00 a week for psychotherapy. Through the ministry of Victory in Jesus, the healing process in his life finally began.

He told me, "It's hard to understand all this. I can't believe how much money I was spending each week. Then I come to a simple meeting like this and hear words from the Bible, and I am set free. The Word of God showed me that I live in two different worlds. It showed me that my problem was spiritual, not psychological."

Through the process of healing that began in Victory in Jesus, this attorney was able to put his medication aside and begin living a life of victory.

"For the Word of God is quick and powerful, and sharper than any twoedged sword, piercing even to the dividing asunder of soul and spirit, and of the joints and marrow, and is a discerner of the thoughts and intents of the heart" (Heb 4:12).

Free Indeed !

"If the Son therefore shall make you free, ye shall be free indeed" (John 8:36). This is the experience of so many former enslaved victims who have come through our Victory in Jesus ministry. What joy it brings to my heart as I reflect on these individuals—more trophies of God's grace and love. Their faces flash before me as I write, and my heart is warmed by the precious memories they represent.

For example, a young man named Bill, a former heroin addict who was on methadone therapy, came to our services at Faith Fellowship. His methadone addiction had lasted for fifteen years. After he received Jesus in a church service, it was my privilege to pray with him in the prayer room.

After a time of warring prayer, I announced to Bill that he had been set free.

He asked, "You mean I'm set free from methadone?"

The enemy had lied to him, saying that he would have to take methadone for the rest of his life. This is why Bill was so stunned by my announcement of faith. The best that society could do for him was to substitute one drug addiction for another.

I reiterated my announcement to him, "Yes, Bill, you have been set free from methadone. I believe what I said when I prayed."

"You mean I don't have to go and get methadone tomorrow?"

"Instead of me telling you that, Bill, I'll let the Word of God reassure you." I turned to Galatians 5:1 and read, "Stand fast therefore in the liberty wherewith Christ made us free, and be not entangled again with the yoke of bondage."

Bill told me he would stand on that promise. The next day the nurse from the treatment center called him to ask why he has missed his apointment. He told her, " I don't need it anymore. Jesus has set me free."

The nurse laughed sarcastically and said, "You're crazy!" Then she hung up on him.

It was his first experience with persecution after becoming a Christian, but he responded to it with faith, courage, and hope. Bill was determined to keep on keeping on. As a result of the choice he made, the extent of discomfort Bill experienced amounted to a few sleepless nights. That's God.

But Bill's deliverance didn't end there. His wife was a denominational Christian who began to marvel at the extraordinary change she noticed in her husband. It was so hard for her to understand. She had known him as a drug addict for so many years. She was at a loss to account for the changes in her husband.

Their daughter, Carolyn, had some developmental problems, and she was unable to speak. "If God can heal Carolyn, I'll come to your church," she told her husband.

The next Sunday Bill came to church with his little seven-year-old girl. He stopped me in the hall, and told me what his wife had said. I responded simply by placing my hands over Carolyn's ears. Then I bound the evil spirit and loosed it from the child's body and thanked God for opening her ears and teaching her to speak.

That week Carolyn went to school. Her teacher called Bill's wife and said, " What happened to Carolyn? We can't stop her from talking!"

It has been more than eight years since Bill and Carolyn were set free. His wife and his entire family now attend Faith Fellowship. There is no more methadone. They live in a new house, drive a new car, and celebrate a new life together. They are free indeed !

No One Is Beyond Hope

Pedophiles are people (usually men) who sexually abuse children. Child abusers are both victimizers and victims of the enemy. Most of these individuals are looked upon by society as the lowest of the low for understandable reasons. It is believed they are beyond hope, doomed to a life of incarceration and/or a continuing practice of this perversion.

We've had several of these men attend Victory in Jesus meetings awaiting sentences for their crimes. Like the drug addict or alcoholic, the pedophile is an addict. His particular propensity is young children, sometimes his own children or the children of relatives.

John was one such individual. He came to Victory in Jesus at the insistence of his wife. In addition to this sexual addiction, John was a heavy drinker and a drug addict who weighed over 250 pounds.

On the particular Friday evening in question, as I began to minister the Word of God, I noticed this man sitting at the back of the room. His face really stood out to me.

The Holy Spirit interrupted me in the middle of my message by saying, *Vinny, call him up, I want to set him free.*

"Jesus," I replied inwardly, "do you see the size of that man?" He was well over six-feet-tall and carried his weight in an intimidating manner. I wrestled with my orders for only a few moments, but I kept being drawn back to the man sitting at the back of the room. I walked toward him and commanded, "Stand up! Jesus is going to set you free tonight."

John did stand. I laid my hands on him, and in that instant of time, he was set completely free. From then on, John attended our meetings regularly for about a year. Then he was sentenced to serve three years of a four-year sentence at the state penitentiary for sex offenders in Avenel, New Jersey. He went into prison a free man!

Before he was sentenced, his wife stopped me to say, "Brother Vinny, God gave me a new husband. I had learned to live with his drug addiction and other habits, but when he was set free I had to learn to live with a man I didn't know." John was a completely new creation in Christ Jesus.

Pedophiles, like many other types of addicts, wrestle with feelings of low self esteem. Most of the time they hate themselves for what they do. They would like to be able to control their behavior, but they feel powerless to do so. Demonic powers of darkness continue their task assignment on the lives of these men, causing them to feel like total failures.

Such was the case with a a young man named Scott. I assured him that God was aware of his problem and that He was ministering to him in that area. It was his job, I pointed out, to remain persistent by acting upon the faith that is imparted by the Word of God. Scott did so, and eventually he disclosed his problem to me of his own volition.

We maintain a standard at Victory in Jesus never to inquire as to why anyone attends. There is no need for anyone to know what the problem is, because God knows it. Being there is the important thing. However, when Scott freely chose to confess this sin to me, this act released it, and Scott was healed. The biblical precedent for this approach is found in James: "And the prayer of faith shall save the sick, and the Lord shall raise him up; and if he has committed sins, they shall be forgiven him. Confess your faults one to another, and pray one for another that ye may be healed. The effectual fervent prayer of a righteous man availeth much" (James 5:15-16).

HIV

We hear much about AIDS in the media. It has affected every strata of society. Millions are infected world-wide. Some of these victims have come to Victory in Jesus, seeking hope and help.

Edwin was one such individual. He became a Christian after living as a Muslim with the name of Mohammed. When he became a Christian he reverted to his birth name. Edwin was delivered from intravenous drug use in 1989, but he found out he was HIV-positive. After he received Jesus, he was rushed to the hospital that same week. His lung X-rays revealed an infection. Edwin wept profusely as he called me to share these things. "They're going to admit me, " he explained. "Brother Vinny, they say my lungs are infected. I'm so scared."

"Wait a minute, Edwin, here's what we're gonna do. We're gonna pray and take authority over all of this, in the name of Jesus. Are you ready?"

"Okay, " Edwin responded.

I could almost hear Edwin brace himself for the words that were about to be said. The ensuing prayer over the phone rebuked the lie of the enemy, and I commanded Edwin's lungs to be healed. I felt the power of God literally burst from me through the telephone lines to Edwin who was in the hospital awaiting admission. I thanked God for making him completely whole in Jesus' name.

"Edwin, now I want you to ask your doctors to take another X-ray before admitting you to the hospital."

"Okay, Brother Vinny, I will."

He called me later to tell me that everything was okay. He told me that the doctor could not believe the difference between the second set of X-rays and the first set. He called in another specialist who said, "This is totally confusing."

Edwin responded to the doctors, "You guys are confused, so I'm going home."

Regrettably I cannot report that Edwin maintained his freedom and his healing. He ended up going back to his old habits. This happened because he stopped attending Victory in Jesus meetings too early, before he was adequately built up in the Word of God. Before long, I heard he was using drugs again, and my heart grieved for him.

Some months later a friend of Edwin's called me. "He's back in the hospital, Vinny."

I had not seen Edwin for several months. When I got to the hospital, I could not believe the change that had taken place in his body. He was lying in his bed, so emaciated that he was obviously near death.

He looked at me pathetically and said, "Brother Vinny, I can't take it no more; I just want to leave."

I understood what he was telling me as I ministered restoration and reconciliation to him. Though Edwin had been saved, his mind had not been renewed. His experience was one of those that led Nancy and me to reexamine our ministry in 1989. God showed us that the battle is within the soul or the mind of the new believer. We knew the strong man in charge of the individual's life has to be expelled, because in Edwin's case the strongman won. He had gotten away with his destructive plan. He had merely sacrificed an underling spirit of infirmity under his authority so he could remain behind to call his troops back into Edwin's life.

God's Rest

God wants His people to rest in Him. "Let us therefore fear, lest, a promise being left us of entering his rest, any of you should come short of it. For unto us was the gospel preached, as well as unto them: but the word preached did not profit them, not being mixed with faith in them that heard it" (Heb. 4:1-2).

God's rest comes when the Word of God is mixed with faith. When we take what we have learned from submitting to God's Word and obediently apply this knowledge to our lives, there is great profit for us. God has ordained this to be so. Conversely, the Word of God does not profit an individual, even though God designs it for profit, if the individual does not forcefully apply this new-found knowledge he came to believe by faith into his life. This is a personal choice which makes or breaks the person down the road. We are warned by the Lord to "Enter in through the narrow gate: for wide is the gate and spacious and broad that leads away to destruction, and many are those who are entering through it" (Matt. 7:13 TAB).

Jesus said, "Have the faith of God" (Mark 11:22). This is the answer. This is the key to finding rest from the warfare. This is the victory that overcomes the world. After we have taken authority, we can rest in Him and be confident that He will perform His Word.

"For verily I say unto you, That whosoever shall say unto this mountain, Be thou removed, and cast into the sea; and shall not doubt in his heart, but shall believe that those things which he saith shall come to pass; he shall have whatsoever he saith. Therefore I say unto you, What things so ever ye desire, when ye pray, believe that ye receive them, and ye shall have them" (Mark 11:23-24).

Hope that is seen does not work. This is why twelve-step programs and other secular approaches fall short of the glory of God and fail to meet the needs of the human heart. "For we are saved by hope: but hope that is seen is not hope: for what a man seeth, why doth he yet hope for? But if we hope for that we see not [through faith in the Word], then do we with patience wait for it" (Rom. 8:24-25).

Patience is part of the healing process. It is mingled with trust and faith. "Now faith is the substance of things hoped for, the evidence of things not seen" (Heb 11:1).

In making these observations, it is not my desire to put down or discount the work of doctors, counselors, helping professionals, rehab programs, and other attempts to help. I thank God for secular programs, because so many people are in trouble that we need them! I'm simply saying that for Christians, similar approaches are made complete when they incorporate faith in God and the knowledge of God's spiritual dimension into their practice. Christians need more than an acknowledgement of some sort of benign "power that is greater than ourselves" for victory. Christians need to tap into their heritage, that power which is released by God through His Word. This is the way to God's rest without stress.

"For thus said the Lord God, the Holy One of Israel: In returning and resting you shall be saved; in quietness and in confidence shall be your strength . . ." (Isa. 30:15).

11

No Fear !

There is no fear is love; but perfect love casteth
out fear; because
fear hath torment. He that feared is not made
perfect in love. We love
him, because he first loved us.
(1 John 4:18-19)

Fear Is Death's Fuel

The enemy of our souls seeks to devour and destroy us by any means available to him. Many times he will use fear, beginning in the soul realm of our thought-life, to bring this to pass. Such fear, however, does not have any power over us unless we start to entertain it in our thoughts.

People who are fearful may have been traumatized when they were young. Perhaps they were abandoned, abused, or rejected. Whatever the cause, such deep inner hurts in our formative years make us insecure and vulnerable.

Many of the people we work at Victory in Jesus come from such backgrounds. They are filled with anxiety and insecurity. One of these, a young woman named Betty (who was destined to play a personal role in our lives), had been put up for adoption by her birth mother when she was very young. She lived with her adoptive parents and grandparents in a home that adhered to a denominational teaching.

Her grandfather died when she was five, leaving her ailing grandmother in the care of Becky's adoptive mother. This meant that family outings were no longer possible, and her mother had to give most of her attention to her grandmother. These factors created a lot of stress and strain in their family relationships, and before long, her adoptive parents began to quarrel frequently.

Materially, Betty did not lack very many things. She had nice clothing, her own TV, a stereo, a telephone, and many other possessions. Something was lacking, however, and that was her need for love. Her grandmother grew increasingly ill, and when Betty was eleven, her grandmother died.

The death of Betty's grandmother was more than her mother could bear. She became very emotionally distraught and more distant than ever. In a subconscious reaction to the lack of love at home, Betty began to seek love and affection from boys in her peer group. She began attending parties where alcohol and marijuana were freely available. Her striving for popularity and acceptance led her to experiment with cigarettes, beer, and marijuana.

After high school she attended a school for models and soon met an attractive young man who was twenty-one. She found him interesting for several reasons, especially because he was three years older than her. Betty and

David began dating secretly. School became less significant to her at this time, and she began cutting classes and doing poorly in her subjects. Smoking pot and drinking were integral parts of their relationship.

When Betty's parents discovered their relationship, they forbade her to see David. She was not about to abide by this restriction, so she and David ran away together. Her parents reported her absence to the police, and by the time Betty was found she was using cocaine, speed, and acid. She spent the weekend after the police found her in a juvenile detention center, which Betty found to be both degrading and humiliating.

She said, "I was so scared. I had never experienced anything like this. I had only seen it in movies. I felt humiliated and degraded. I felt that I was better than that, that I did not deserve to be in a cell!"

The judge ruled that she should go home as she was not yet eighteen. Back home, the tension seemed unbearable to Betty. Her parents didn't trust her and she felt completely miserable. Finally, her dad told her that she could leave if she wanted to, but with only the clothes on her back. Betty chose to leave home once more.

She left everything behind, including the car her parents had provided for her and went to the home of David's parents. She knew she had hurt her parents, but her own interests (and perceived needs) took precedence in her life. Soon thereafter, her dad filed for divorce from her mom.

Betty still found life with David exciting. She thought that he made her feel special. With him, she could get served in bars and have all the drugs she wanted. She soon discovered that her boyfriend was heavily into speed, which had a profound effect upon his personality. Prince Charming became a monster under the influence of this amphetamine. In order to feed his habit, he expected Betty to sell her jewelry so he could purchase more drugs. Once he took all her jewelry and he began to steal from her mother.

Betty went with him to New York City. She describes the experience as follows: "I remember going to a coke-house and seeing people shooting up in their necks. The floors were covered with cockroaches and people were vomiting out of the windows on the seventh floor. I just wanted to get out of there! I couldn't believe that my boyfriend would take me to such a place."

David's behavior toward Betty grew increasingly abusive. "When he was doing speed, he would yell and curse at me in a very mean-spirited way, and then he began to slap me around. Whereas before I had always dressed nicely in the finest designer clothing, I was now wearing old, dirty jeans with holes in them. I couldn't use make-up because I couldn't afford it and my hair was unkempt. My self-esteem was deteriorating."

Betty was eighteen years old when she discovered she was pregnant. "I was so scared. I had never even held a baby. David wanted me to abort it, but I knew I couldn't do that. I was still smoking cigarettes, doing coke, and now and then, I would take a hit of mescaline. Finally, when I was in my fifth month, I went to see a doctor. David wouldn't let me see my mother or other family members, and he continued to abuse me. Finally, when I was eight months pregnant, I went to see my mother."

Betty became so terrified and paranoid that she felt totally isolated from everyone. She writes, "The night I went into labor I will never forget. David was up and snorting coke until 4:00 am. I woke up at 5:30 and ate a can of cold beets. Then I went back to bed, but the pains began shortly thereafter. I had to wake David up so he could take me to the hospital. He was mad. He said, 'If you don't have that baby, I'm going to kick your butt all the way home from the hospital !' I was crying because I was so afraid."

Her baby, little Jennifer, was born on February 16, 1983. Betty said, "I can remember calling out to God and asking Him to let me have a healthy baby (with ten fingers and ten toes)—completely normal in every respect. Thank God, He answered my prayer."

When she got home from the hospital, her situation with David was still the same, even worse. "We lost our apartment because David had used the money for drugs. We were evicted—a new baby and no home! "

It never really was a home for Betty or the baby. While she lived there, she was frequently beaten by David. On the night of Jennifer's baptism, for example, David gave her a black eye !

Everything continued to get worse. David grew paranoid and thought that Betty was being unfaithful to him. Once he kicked her down a flight of stairs, and she had to spend time recovering from her injuries in the hospital. Her doctor warned her, " You need to get out of this relationship before it is too late for you!"

A friend encouraged Betty to leave David and to begin working as a nightclub dancer. She followed the friend's advice after moving home with her mother, and Betty began dancing in different clubs. This gave her both attention and money. She began earning more than $200.00 per night. Her mother did not approve of this new life-style, so she was forced to leave home again. Betty and Jennifer moved in with a friend who had encouraged her to leave David and begin dancing.

She began dating different guys and continuing with the drug scene. She soon married a man named Greg, who seemed to care about her and Jennifer. They had a baby named Jesse who had some physical problems. Jesse needed surgery when he was only six weeks old due to a blockage in his small intestine. Around the same time, Betty's mother was saved and she began telling her daughter about Jesus.

The prayers of God's people for little Jesse were heard and answered. He went through the surgery successfully. Meanwhile, Betty's mom continued to encourage her to attend church. She came to Victory in Jesus meetings once in a while in order to keep her mother quiet.

Betty explains, "I would hear the message but I would always manage to leave before the altar call was given. I met Vinny and Nancy Longo and I can remember Nancy cornering me by the stairway and telling me to let go and let God. She explained that God had a plan for my life. While she was talking, though, I wasn't even able to look at her.

It was a time of increasing restlessness in Betty's life. She drank and used drugs ever more heavily. She began to run—from what she did not seem to know, but most likely it was God. The Hound of Heaven was pursuing her. She went to Hawaii to be with Greg. Then they moved to Florida.

Eventually, she left him and returned to New Jersey. She began dancing again. Her cocaine habit was costing over $200.00 a day, and her mother noticed the downward spiral in Betty's life.

Her mother's intervention led to Jennifer being placed with her while Jesse was put into a home for foster children. This got Betty's attention for a while, but it was not enough to set her on the right track. She said, "My life was devastated. I felt I had nothing without my children because they were what I lived for."

Nonetheless she went on with drugs, dancing, and a new boyfriend, who was a dealer. She would party for days at a time. She hardly ever ate. She would do coke and then drink to bring her down. Her friends had to literally force her to eat. She describes this time in her life as follows: " I hated my life. I wasn't able to see my kids except for supervised visits. My mom would no longer help me, but she would tell me I needed to turn to God. She explained to me that this was all she could do for me. She said she had given me to God, and He would take good care of me. Though I did not understand what she meant, it sounded sort of peaceful to me.

"One night in a bar I saw a nice man I had met three years previously. I knew he was married and I wasn't interested in married men. He was a nice guy, however, and he seemed interested in talking to me. He explained that he was in the process of a divorce. There seemed to be something very special about him and I liked him very much.

"I found out that he and I had something in common. He explained that his father was a minister who ran a ministry called Victory in Jesus. I told him I had attended some of their meetings in the past, and then I told him about the lady with reddish hair who had counseled with me there. That woman—Nancy Longo—was his mom!

"It seemed like an uncanny coincidence. The young man's name was John Banks, and I began to really like him. We began to see each other frequently—and even began going to church together. At the same time, however, we continued to drink, do drugs, and smoke cigarettes—that is until we started going to Victory in Jesus meetings and attending all the regular services of the church. The conviction of the Holy Ghost got us, and we realized we couldn't continue with life as it always had been. Almost together, we made a solid commitment to Jesus Christ."

The power of God began to work in the lives of Betty and John. They were completely set free from drugs and alcohol. As time went on, John and Betty got married and had a baby, Alicia. At first, they lived with Nancy and me. It was a time of rejoicing for us, as we realized once again that God had proven His faithfulness to us. He had heard and answered our prayers for our family. It was such a joy to see them learn to stand on the Word of God for themselves. They faced some difficulties, especially related to their battle to regain custody of Jesse, but God was faithful. What a joy they are to us, and all of our grandchildren fill us with tender love and contentment.

Truly, God's perfect love does cast out all fear, because we know that He knows what we have need of even before we express it to Him (See Luke 12:30-32). .He wants to bless us, and He promises to reward us if we will have faith in Him (See Heb. 11).

Betty had to learn all this the hard way, but she now knows, first-hand, that ". . . fear hath torment. He that feareth is not made perfect in love" (1 John 4:18). The devil wants to get us stuck in fear because he knows we're powerless when we're afraid. Fear literally immobilizes us; it keeps us from experiencing any of the good things God has for us.

Betty's fear of rejection caused her to surrender her judgment, her health, her happiness, and everything else to men that she thought loved her. Each of these relationships, until she met John and they found victory in Jesus, was an unhealthy codependent addiction. Thank God, Betty found Jesus before it was too late for her and her children. Now they know God's perfect love, which casts out all fear.

Free From Fear

"Your Father knoweth that ye have need of these things. But rather seek ye the kingdom of God; and all these things shall be added unto you. Fear not, little flock; for it is your Father's good pleasure to give you the kingdom" (Luke 12:30-32).

The enemy wants us to be fearful, but our Father wants us to rest in Him. If we seek Him and His righteousness first, we need have no fear about anything (See Matt. 6:33). Once, while on a crusade with our church in Jamaica, we were ministering on a flat-body truck that we were using as a platform in the middle of town. We were involved in street evangelism, and we had a Christian band that God would use to gather the crowds around us. One of our musicians, a guitar player, had been a Rastafarian before he became a Christian.

While the music was playing, I went out into the assembled crowd in order to witness to the people. A pot-smoking Rastafarian approached me with an angry demeanor and began to scream at me with profanity and hateful insults. I noticed that he began to search his pocket as if he were reaching to pull something out. I was sure he had a concealed weapon.

The guitar player took note of what was happening. He jumped off the truck in order to intervene in this potentially tragic situation. I stopped him, "You are not going to sign my death warrant! I trust in God."

219

The guitar player had fear written all over his face, but I felt a great peace even though the deranged Rastafarian was by now right in my face. By faith, I claimed an invisible, impenetrable barrier between us. I claimed it audibly, and the Rastafarian seemed amazed as I rubbed the invisible shield with my hands as if I could actually feel it.

The evil man seemed totally immobilized. He could not even lift his hand from his pocket! His face had become a maze of confusion. He could not speak as we faced each other, eyeball to eyeball. Even the stream of profanity from his lips had been blocked by the invisible shield I had erected by faith. I took authority in the spirit over the potentially harmful situation, because I knew the truth of Isaiah's words. "No weapon formed against thee shall prosper; and every tongue that shall rise against thee in judgment thou shalt condemn. This is the heritage of the servants of the Lord, and their righteousness is of Me, saith the Lord" (Isa. 54:17).

God never fails us when we place our total faith in Him. He is our shield and our buckler. "The Lord is my light and my salvation, whom shall I fear: The Lord is the strength of my life; of whom shall I be afraid? . . . Though an host should encamp against me, my heart shall not fear" (Ps. 27:1-3).

The Great Counterfeiter

Satan is a liar; in fact, he is the father of lies. He is the accuser of the brethren. When Jesus stands at the door of our hearts and knocks, Satan will do everything within his power to keep us from opening the door to the One who has all power in heaven and on earth. That's because the devil is afraid of Jesus. Being so familiar with fear, therefore, it is not surprising that the enemy will try to use fear to trip us up.

The lies may say, "Don't let Jesus in. If you do, you will have to surrender all your happiness." "Look at all the hypocrites in the church. Why would you want to be like them?" "God is not real." "Don't be stupid. If you become a Christian, look at all you will have to give up." And on and on they go.

When a knock comes on the door of our hearts once we have been delivered, we must be very careful to be sure that we don't open the door to the wrong visitor. The devil, as we have already shown, will try to regain entrance. He will bring other evil spirits with him. This is why it is so essential for every believer to renew his or her mind with the washing in the water of the Word of God. It is this renewal that helps us to distinguish between the truth and a lie. This renewal helps us to join our thoughts with God's. The renewal of our mind helps us to know the will of God. When we know the truth, it sets us free from all fear and manipulation on the part of the enemy. Whose voice are we listening to?

"My sheep hear my voice, and I know them, and they follow me" (John 10:27). When Jesus announced to His disciples that He would have to stand trial in Jerusalem, Peter protested. Jesus knew that Peter was speaking the devil's lie so He said, "Get thee behind me, Satan." When the devil lies to us we must do the same. Peter pitied Jesus, but Jesus knew that self-pity is of the devil, and He wanted nothing to do with that form of evil. Peter had manifested Satan's lying voice through his own, and Jesus rebuked the lie.

Ultimately these issues are a matter of personal choice. The natural mind says, "I'm on my own in this situation. I will decide."

The spiritual mind, on the other hand, says, "God intervenes in my behalf." Notice how Paul paints this contrast in Romans 8: "For to be carnally minded is death; but to be spiritually minded is life and peace" (Rom. 8:6).

The Word of God renews our minds in such a way that we can receive spiritual life that is abundant and full of glory. In the face of difficult circumstances it always says, "God will intervene on my behalf." As the Lord went before the Israelites in battle, so will He do with us. He gave them the victory, and He wants us to lead victorious lives as well. The Lord intervenes in every situation in a spiritual way; the physical part is just to pick up the spoils that remain behind after the enemy surrenders.

Under the Shadow of the Almighty

"He that dwelleth in the secret place of the most high shall abide under the shadow of the Almighty. I will say o the Lord, He is my refuge and my fortress: my God; in Him will I trust. Surely He shall deliver thee from the snare of the fowler, and from the noisome pestilence. He shall cover thee with his feathers, and under His wings shalt thou trust: His truth shall be thy shield and buckler. Thou shall not be afraid for the terror by night; nor the arrow that flies by day" (Ps. 91:1-5).

Our safe place is found under the wings of the Almighty God. "For though we walk in the flesh, we do not war after the flesh: (For the weapons of our warfare are not carnal, but mighty through God to the pulling down of strongholds;) Casting down imaginations, and every high thing that exalts itself against the knowledge of God, and bringing into captivity every thought, to the obedience of Christ" (2 Cor. 10:3-5).

When we fight in the realms of our mind or flesh we always fail, but if we trust in God to do battle for us we become winners. God responds to our faith by bringing about manifestations of victory in the physical and soulish realms of our lives as well as the spiritual.

One young lady we had the privilege of ministering to is named Pamela. She had been repeatedly raped by her own father from the age of nine years on. When she was thirteen she ran away from home. A well-dressed couple found her, and recognizing that she was a runaway who had the innocent look of a child, they took control of her life. They knew that Pamela was just the kind of kid they were looking for to help them in their drug trade. They took her in, showered affection on her, and then began to use her. They would strap drugs to her body, underneath her clothing. Then they would put her with a well-dressed couple who would sometimes have a younger child with them as well. They looked like an all-American family going on vacation.

On one of these occasions, Pamela had over $180,000 worth of cocaine on her, and the other child who was with them must have been carrying a similar quantity. After using her in this way (and sexually abusing her as well), they let Pamela go. By now she had lost that innocent look on her face. Somehow she ended up in New Orleans, and she had become a child of the streets, along with many other children and teen-agers who had been left alone in the city. She soon discovered that many of these kids had stolen for drug dealers and carried drugs for them even as she had done.

Pamela and her peers had lost their identities. They had become jaded at very young ages. They had learned to cover over their fear with cynicism. Many of them had been so young when they were captured that they literally forgot who they were or where they had come from. Most of them got picked up by pimps who became their "father figures." Pamela was one of these unfortunate victims of our society as well.

She went into prostitution for a short while in order to have enough money to survive. Her initial plan was to turn only one trick, but soon prostitution became her life-style, and drugs kept her under the pimp's satanic control. Pamela, at the age of fourteen, remembered her mother. She called home, "Mom, things are happening to me. I need help."

Her mother's reply crushed her down even further, "Things are better here without you."

Rejection upon rejection. Her only friend seemed to be the drugs. Everyone else used her for what they wanted.

Eventually a pimp became her husband. Though both of them received Jesus Christ as their Savior, the pimp died of AIDS early in their marriage. They had a daughter, and Pamela and her baby were left alone. It was another form of rejection for her. Pamela had trusted Christ for salvation, but she was leading a defeated Christian life, without hope. Pamela still didn't know who she was in Christ, and upon finding the house empty, the unclean spirit who used to live in her returned and brought another set of evil spirits who were under his command, including the fear of eating. This developed into anorexia, bulimia, and other eating disorders. These addictions replaced the drugs and prostitution that had dominated her life for so long.

Eventually she found her way back to New Jersey, where she started attending Victory in Jesus meetings. She didn't really feel comfortable in the services because the darkness that was still in her life was afraid of the light that shone in the meetings. The light of God is intense, and it dissipates the darkness. The brighter it gets the more uncomfortable all darkness becomes, until finally it has to leave.

It is comparable to what happens when we lift a rock that is buried in a field. The insects that live beneath it begin to flee, because they prefer the cold darkness to the warm light. People are like this too, especially if they are used to the darkness. "In the beginning was the Word, and the Word was with God and the Word was God. The same was in the beginning with God. All things were made by Him; and without Him was not anything made that was made. In Him was life; and the life was the light of men. And the light shineth in darkness; and the darkness comprehended it not" (John 1:1-5). The Apostle goes on, "He came unto His own, and His own received Him not. But as many as received Him, to them gave He power to become Sons of God, even to them that believe on His name" (John 1:11-12).

In Pamela's case, God's grace enabled her to overcome the darkness and find her total deliverance. First, however, she spent some time in a mental hospital. When she was discharged, God moved into her life and set her free from the eating disorders and the fear that she had known all her life.

Her outward appearance changed accordingly as she was renewed by the Word of God. Her short, tight dresses were replaced by more modest clothing, and eventually she joined the staff of Victory in Jesus. Now, she has a special ministry to women that have been sexually abused.

Fear of Exposure

Through our work with Victory in Jesus we have learned that there are many "hidden Christians" who are suffering in silence as they lead double lives with one foot in church and one in the world. These men and women are sexually tormented individuals.

We've discovered that many battle with pornography leading to engage in self-abuse and/or illicit sex. Some are involved in indecent exposure, voyeurism, and other activities of darkness. They do not realize that they are captive to the devices of the kingdom of Satan, who is the deceiver. They struggle in a sea of guilt and despair, and are completely ignorant of the power of God. They fear exposure to their family and friends.

Late one evening a man who refused to give his name called me, "Vinny, I attend Victory in Jesus, but I don't have victory in a certain area of my life. I find myself looking at commercials with seductive women and sexual scenes on TV and then I head to the bathroom to masturbate."

As we talked, I learned that he had been exposed to masturbation as a young boy when he discovered his father's magazines in a bureau. He was so ashamed of himself. The devil had routed him into a corner.

He went on to tell me, "Every time I go past an adult bookstore I have to stop. There's a compulsion that drives me there every single time. I will usually buy a video, take it home, look at it, and then burn it. I'm so ashamed of myself for this."

"You need to come back to Victory in Jesus," I told him. "You need to have your mind renewed. Even though you burn the pornographic videos after you watch them, the damage is done. The unclean spirit is satisfied. He has to be dethroned."

Before long the man came to me at one of our meetings and told me that he was the one who had called. I told him, "You left too soon. What you need to do is buy one of our videos and keep playing it until your mind is renewed."

"Yes, you're right," he answered, and then he went to the tape counter and purchased one of our videos. He continued coming to Victory in Jesus until he found true victory in Jesus. He was set free. Not long thereafter, he was married and continues to live in victory.

"A double minded man is unstable in all his ways" (James 1:8), but a mind that is renewed by the Word of God has no fear.

Change Is Painful

God wants us to change. He wants us to know that we're complete in Christ. Most people, however, resist change because it goes against the grain of human nature. We become complacent with life, and we seek to follow the path of least resistance because change is painful.

There are five points that must be taken into consideration as we take steps toward positive change in our lives. These are clearly outlined for us in Colossians 1:10-11: "That ye might walk worthy of the Lord unto all pleasing, being fruitful in every good work, and increasing in the knowledge of God; Strengthened with all might,

227

according to his glorious power, unto all patience and longsuffering with joyfulness."

Point One—We must walk worthy of the Lord unto all pleasing.

Point Two—We must be fruitful in every good work.

Point Three—We must continue to increase in the knowledge of God.

Point Four—We must be strengthened with all might according to His glorious power.

Point Five—We must exhibit patience and long-suffering with joyfulness.

These are God's goals for us, and when we begin to operate in all five points we know we are ready to be used in the Master's service by being joined to other believers in a committed fellowship.

Equipping the Saints

Victory in Jesus is not a church. We see ourselves as being more like a front-line operation on the battlefield. We work with the victims of the battle in an effort to bring healing, training, and victory to them. In this way we are preparing them for active participation in the Church of Jesus Christ.

We endeavor to respect the privacy of those who come to us. Confidentiality is extremely important to us. Those who have come out of the battle are so scarred and injured and fearful that it's hard for them to trust people. We must assure them that we can be trusted with their deepest secrets. We tell them that we will not reveal their struggles to others unless they give us permission to do so, and the only time we would seek such permission is if we felt there was someone in our midst who could be helped by their specific testimony.

We teach them the importance of giving. "For God so loved the world, that he *gave* His only begotton Son, that whosoever believeth in Him should not perish, but have everlasting life" (John 3:16, italics mine). "Freely ye have received, freely give" (Matt. 10:8).

We give them intensive teaching from the Word of God. We point them to Jesus, the Author and Finisher of our faith, and we make every effort to build them up in the faith that was once delivered unto the saints (See Hebs. 12:2, Jude 3).

Keep the Emphasis on the Word of God

"Thus saith the Lord; Cursed be the man that trusteth in man, and maketh flesh his arm, and whose hearth departeth from the Lord" (Jer. 17:5). We need to trust God, to have faith in Him, to take him at His Word, to believe His precepts.

"Blessed is the man that walketh not in the council of the ungodly, nor standeth in the way of sinners, nor sitteth in the seat of the scornful. But his delight is in the law of the Lord; and in His law doth he meditate day and night. And he shall be like a tree planted by the rivers of living water, that bringeth forth his fruit in his season; his leaf also shall not wither; and whatsoever he doeth shall prosper" (Ps. 1:1-3).

"Wherewithal shall a young man cleanse his way? by taking heed thereto according to thy word . . . thy word have I hid in mine heart, that I might not sin against thee" (Ps. 119:9-11).

"All scripture is given by inspiration of God, and is profitable for doctrine, for reproof, for correction, for instruction in righteousness: That the man of God may be perfect, thoroughly furnished unto all good works" (2 Tim. 3:16).

Realizing that our responsibility is a very serious one, we never encourage those who come to Victory in Jesus to rely on us. The arm of flesh fails, but Jesus never fails. Therefore, we keep on pointing them to Him and His Word. God spoke these words very clearly to my heart, *Vinny, never take the emphasis away from My Word. Always keep the emphasis on My Word. If you do this, I'll fight you're battles. Anyone who comes against you is coming against me.*

This, my friends, is the key to Victory in Jesus. Heaven and earth may pass away, but God's Word never changes.

Epilogue

We trust that the teachings and testimonies we've shared with you on the pages of this book have helped you to see that there is victory in Jesus. He is the answer, no matter what the question. Nancy and I have learned through so many experiences in our life and ministry that God can be trusted implicitly in every area of our life.

Nothing is too hard for Him. He loves you, and He wants to prosper you and lead you into the glorious liberty of the sons of God. Faith is the key that unlocks the door to all He has for you. His treasure chest is overflowing with so many good things for you.

We have surrendered our lives to God. Where He leads us we will follow. We would counts it a privilege to bring God's Word to your church or area. To contact us please write:

Victory In Jesus Outreach Ministries
P.O. Box 11023
New Brunswick, N J 08906

Believe and receive victory in Jesus for your life right now. He truly is able to do exceeding, abundantly above all that you can ask or think, according to the power that works in you. Unto Him be the glory in the church by Christ Jesus throughout all ages, world without end. Amen (Paraphrased from Ephesians 3:20-21). This is our prayer for you.

There is no fear - absolutely no fear - when we are walking hand in hand with Jesus and standing on the promises of His Word. "Because thous hast made the Lord, which is my refuge, even the Most High, thy habitation; There shall no evil befall thee, neither shall any plague come nigh thy dwelling. For he shall give his angels charge over thee, to keep thee in all thy ways. They shall bear you up in their hands, lest thou dash thy foot against a stone. Thou shalt tread upon the lion and the adder: the young lion and the dragon shalt thou trample under thy feet. Because he has set his love upon Me, therefore will I deliver him. I will set him on high, because he hath known my name. He shall call upon me, and I will answer him: I will be with him in trouble;I will deliver him, and honour him. With long life will I satisfy him, and show him my salvation" (Ps. 91:9-16).